THEME
AND
PARAGRAPH

THEME
AND
PARAGRAPH

Philip Burnham

Richard Lederer

St. Paul's School
Concord, New Hampshire

A Basic Verbal Skills Book

Independent School Press

Wellesley Hills   Massachusetts

The authors and publishers thank Scott, Foresman & Company for permission to use some material originally in their copyright. Such material has been revised and brought up to date by the authors.

CONTENTS

PREFACE

The special concern of *Theme and Paragraph* is the teaching of composition skills that will be most useful for students in grades 7-12. The "Speaking and Writing" section presents eight basic types of composition: narration (Telling What Happened), description (Telling How Something Looks), character study (Telling about Interesting People), exposition (Telling How Something is Made or Done), explanation of an abstract term (Telling What Something Means), opinion based on reasons (Expressing an Opinion), preference based on a comparison (Expressing a Preference), persuasion (Persuading Others).

Two closely integrated lessons in each Unit present a step-by-step explanation of each of these basic types. The first lesson — concerned with thinking and planning — helps the student select a suitable topic, choose and arrange details effectively, determine good beginning and ending sentences, and prepare useful notes for an oral composition. The second lesson, on writing and revising, explains how students can convert their notes into first-draft paragraphs and then how to revise, title, and proofread the written composition. In both lessons specific examples are used to show exactly what the problems are and how they might be solved. In each assignment the examples used and the suggestions made are designed to encourage students to talk and write about subjects of greatest interest to them — their own experiences, interests, observations, ambitions, opinions and work.

Students are seldom at a loss for things to say about themselves and their personal interests. Their weakness, revealed in so many oral talks and written compositions, is often not lack of ideas, but lack of skill in organizing. *Theme and Paragraph* teaches outlining (a simple two-level grouping) as an integral part of the composition process. By stressing the effective organization of ideas by means of specific examples illustrating the grouping of details in time, space, and logical orders, *Theme and Paragraph* creates an awareness of how paragraphs are developed. The lessons attempt to show how unity and coherence are achieved through careful planning and the use of topic sentences, indications of point of view, and transitional expressions.

The second section of *Theme and Paragraph* deals with Paragraph Study. By observing the various functions sentences may have in a paragraph, the ways in which the paragraphs in a composition are linked together, the importance of using space wisely, the uses of special paragraphs (introductory, summarizing, transitional), the student will learn — from concrete examples instead of from abstract discussion — just what unity and coherence and emphasis mean.

Following each discussion in "Working with Paragraphs" is a section called "Improving Paragraphs." Here students are given specific suggestions for using what they have learned in revising their own paragraphs for greater effectiveness.

Phillip Burnham
Richard Lederer

I. SPEAKING AND WRITING:
A Sequence

Presenting Your Work

Unit 1

How oral compositions should sound

Have you ever heard a talk that sounded something like this?

> Well-uh, one morning last summer, my brother had a bright idea. And-uh since he doesn't have very many of them, we-uh decided not to waste this one. So-uh we packed a lunch of sandwiches and-uh hard-boiled eggs and an apple apiece. Then-uh we set out for the river to rent a boat from old Mr. Hooker. And-uh before the sun had gotten really hot, we were-uh headed upstream toward Hobo Island.

If you have, you know that "uh" is not really a word. You know that it is just a sound. But it is more than that. It is a sign of nervousness, a signal that the speaker is not sure of himself, a warning that he has not thought clearly about what he wants to say.

Probably all of us use "uh" more than we should. We use it in conversation, especially to keep others from interrupting us while we are thinking of something more to say. We use it, too, in answering questions, hoping that a "Why-uh" or a "Well-uh" will give us time to collect our thoughts. These uses, common as they are, often lead to a bad habit—starting to talk before we know what we are going to say.

An oral composition differs from informal talking in several ways. It is thought through in advance. It follows a plan. It may be practiced in private as often as necessary. It is given before an audience that is usually polite enough to let the speaker have his say without interruption. Under these circumstances, there is little, if any, excuse for using "uh." And once you begin to notice how tiresome "uh" becomes in listening to others, you will want to avoid it in your oral compositions.

The remedy is easy: Know in advance exactly how you are going to begin, what you are going to say next, and next, and so on to the end. Then remember this one rule: "When you have finished a sentence, don't make any noise." Simply pause for a moment. This gives your listeners a chance to think about what you have just said. More important, it gives you a chance to think about what you are going to say next. Then say it, beginning with a real word and going straight through the sentence without a single "uh."

How written compositions should look

Not all students have beautiful handwriting. But all students can, with a bit of effort, write legibly. And they can, with a little care, make the final draft of their compositions look attractive as well as neat.

The first page of an ordinary composition should look something like the example at the top of the next page.

Notice the title. It is about an inch and a half from the top of the page and is centered. The first, the last, and all important words are capitalized. There is no punctuation at the end of the title unless it is a question or an exclamation.

A space a line wide is left between the title and the first paragraph. The first word of each paragraph is indented about one inch from the left-hand margin.

Margins about an inch wide at the left and right add to the attractiveness of the page. Keeping the margin at the left is no problem. And by thinking ahead as you write each line and widening or narrowing the spaces between words, you can keep the right margin fairly even. To avoid a ragged appearance at the right, you may have to put part of a word on the next line. If you do, make sure that you divide the word between two syllables and place a hyphen at the end of the line. Consult a dictionary if you are in doubt about where the syllables end. A word of one syllable should never be divided.

If the paper you use is unlined, as this is, leave a space about an inch wide at the bottom. Start the first line of the second page about an inch from the top, not indenting unless you are beginning a new paragraph. If you use lined paper, write on every line of the page before starting another. Begin on the first line of the second page. The first

4

The Better Part of Valor

Here's how it happened. One afternoon, as I was sitting at Joe's lunch counter, munching happily on a thick, juicy hamburger, I heard the sirens. When the Chief's sedan flashed past the window, I grabbed my sandwich and hurried outside to see where the fire was. All I could see was a crowd beginning to gather several blocks down Main Street. Hearing more sirens, I turned in time to see the hook-and-ladder truck swing around the corner and start down Main Street hill. I watched the big truck weave its way down the narrow street between two rows of diagonally parked cars and wondered how it felt to be sitting up there at the rear steering wheel.

Suddenly, about half a block away, a sedan climbed the curb and rolled slowly across the sidewalk. I heard the crash as the car hit the front of a store and shattered a big display window. Then I watched with amazement as the recoil sent the driverless car rolling back across the sidewalk and into its parking place. A moment later a man dashed out of the store, looked wildly up and down the deserted sidewalk, shook his fist angrily in both directions, and darted back into the

page of a composition is not usually numbered, but following pages are. Use Arabic numerals (2, 3, and so on), placing them in the upper right-hand corner.

Telling What Happened

Telling What Happened PART ONE: ORAL

From a classmate's cheery "Hi, Joe. What do you know?" to the newsboy's noisy "Extra! Extra! Read all about it!" people like to hear about happenings that are exciting or amusing or unusual in some way. A newspaper reporter, who earns his living by writing about the doings of other persons, has skill in telling what happened. So has a student who holds the attention of his classmates while telling about something he has done or seen. It is a useful skill, for there are many occasions when we want to share our experiences with others.

For your first composition assignment you are to prepare a short talk about something that you saw happen—an exciting or amusing or unusual occurrence of some sort. You know, of course, that your classmates would be interested in hearing about a thrilling rescue at sea. But your chances of having seen anything that exciting are rather rare. Would it surprise you to learn that your classmates may be just as much interested in your brother's first, clumsy attempt to bake a cake? One of the pleasant things about sharing experiences with the other members of your class is that you do not need something big or unique to talk about. Because they know who you are, they are likely to be interested in almost any amusing or unusual incident that you yourself have actually seen happen.

You will, of course, want to select an incident that is worth telling, something your classmates will enjoy hearing about. What was the most unusual occurrence you ever saw? What strange accident or amusing mishap have you witnessed? What mysterious event or exciting moment can you recall? Be sure to choose an experience

that you think will be likely to interest your class mates. Now what incident will you tell about?

As soon as you have decided on an incident, you can start thinking about the details you will use in telling about it. Exactly what happened? When did it happen, and where? Why were you there? What were you doing? Why did it happen? What was the result? What effect did it have on you? You will find it helpful to list on a piece of scratch paper all the details you can think of. Jot them down quickly as they come to your mind so that you do not forget any of them. Do not worry about the order or wording of the items. A few words for each detail will be enough for a reminder.

When you have completed your list of details, you are ready to make a plan for telling about the incident. This plan should give only the important details. And they should be in the exact order in which they actually occurred. You might begin with where you were or what you were doing just before the incident. Then you would tell what happened first, what happened next, and next, and so on to the end. For example, if you were going to tell about an unusual and rather freakish accident you saw one day, your plan might look like this:

1. Heard sirens as I was sitting at Joe's lunch counter one afternoon
2. Grabbed my sandwich and hurried outside
3. Noticed crowd gathering several blocks down Main Street
4. Heard more sirens and turned to see big hook-and-ladder truck swing around corner and start down Main Street hill
5. Watched it weave its way down the narrow street between rows of diagonally parked cars
6. Wondered what it felt like to be sitting up there at rear steering wheel
7. Suddenly, about half a block away, saw big sedan climb over curb and roll slowly across sidewalk
8. Heard crash as car hit front of store and broke big window
9. Watched with amazement as recoil sent driverless car rolling back across sidewalk and into its parking place
10. A moment later, saw man dash out of store, look wildly up and down the deserted sidewalk, shake his fist angrily in both directions, and dart back into store

11. Smiled at man's helpless rage and tried to figure out what had happened
12. Finally realized that back end of weaving fire truck must have struck rear bumper of car a glancing blow in passing
13. Headed down hill to tell proprietor what only I had seen
14. Found him shouting into telephone: "Yeh, big fellow. Threw bricks or something and broke my window. Want him arrested."
15. Decided to keep quiet and get out of there—fast

The details in this plan are arranged in the order of their occurrence. This is called **time order**. It is the arrangement most often used in telling what happened. Notice that the incident begins with hearing the sirens and that each item following the first adds one or more important details. Keeping the details of an incident in time order makes it easier for others to understand exactly what happened.

Now think carefully about the details in your list. Which ones are essential for understanding what happened? Which ones can be omitted without causing awkward gaps in your account of the incident? Find the first important detail, the one that actually begins the incident. Mark it with a figure 1. Then number the other important details in the order in which they actually occurred. When you have finished, cross off the unnumbered details.

As the talk begins to take shape in your mind, you are ready to think about the opening and closing sentences. If the opening sentence arouses the interest or curiosity of your listeners, they will listen attentively to the details of the incident and know exactly what happened. If the closing sentence brings the incident to a satisfying conclusion, they will feel rewarded for having given you their attention. Knowing how to begin and end your talk effectively is important.

For a talk about the mysterious accident, the opening sentence might be simply the first important detail: "One afternoon, as I was sitting at Joe's lunch counter, munching happily on a big, thick hamburger, I heard the sirens." It might be a short introductory statement intended to arouse interest: "Here's how it happened." Or it might be one intended to arouse curiosity: "I guess I'm the only one who actually saw it happen." Notice that only one introductory statement is used and that it tells just enough to catch the attention of the listeners.

Sometimes a special closing sentence helps to round off the incident, ending it in a satisfying way. It might be a brief explanatory statement: "You never know what a person as excited as that will do." Or it might be a question addressed to the listeners: "What would you have done?" But it must never ramble on and on, and it must never introduce a different topic or a new idea.

How will you begin your talk? When you have decided on an opening sentence, write it at the top of a card or a small piece of paper. Under it write your plan, using only the essential details from your list and putting them down in the order in which you numbered them. Then decide how you will end your talk. Do you need a special closing sentence? If so, write it after the last detail. But if you have difficulty thinking up a brief closing sentence, simply end with the last detail.

These are the notes for your talk. With them in your hand, you will have nothing to be nervous about when you get up to speak.

Be sure to practice your talk at least once before coming to class, timing it to see that you can give it in three minutes or less. Try different ways of telling about the incident, adding any minor details that you think will make it more interesting. But do not try to memorize the talk. Your notes make that unnecessary.

If you are asked to give your talk in class, stand up and wait a moment for everyone to become quiet before you begin speaking.

Telling What Happened PART TWO: WRITTEN

You have prepared a short talk about an exciting or amusing or unusual occurrence that you saw happen. In this assignment you are to write about the same incident. Since the notes you prepared for your talk show you how to begin, what details to give, and how to end, you can concentrate on some of the special problems of written composition: (1) paragraphing, (2) revising, (3) titling, and (4) copying and proofreading your paper before handing it in.

A paragraph usually consists of two or more sentences that are related in meaning. The indention of the first word is a signal to the reader that he is beginning a group of sentences having to do with one part or phase of the topic. During this year you will learn many things about paragraphs, but nothing more important than this: A writer groups sentences together into a paragraph to show his readers that the sentences are related in some way.

For example, if you were going to write about the hook-and-ladder truck that broke a store window, your paragraph plan might look like this:

FIRST PARAGRAPH

OPENING SENTENCE: Here's how it happened.
1. Heard sirens as I was sitting at Joe's lunch counter one afternoon
2. Grabbed my sandwich and hurried outside
3. Noticed crowd gathering several blocks down Main Street
4. Heard more sirens and turned to see big hook-and-ladder truck swing around corner and start down Main Street hill
5. Watched it weave its way down the narrow street between rows of diagonally parked cars
6. Wondered what it felt like to be sitting up there at rear steering wheel

SECOND PARAGRAPH

7. Suddenly, about half a block away, saw big sedan climb over curb and roll slowly across sidewalk
8. Heard crash as car hit front of store and broke big window
9. Watched with amazement as recoil sent driverless car rolling back across sidewalk and into its parking place
10. A moment later, saw man dash out of store, look wildly up and down the deserted sidewalk, shake his fist angrily in both directions, and dart back into store

THIRD PARAGRAPH

11. Smiled at man's helpless rage and tried to figure out what had happened
12. Finally realized that back end of weaving fire truck must have struck rear bumper of car a glancing blow in passing
13. Headed down hill to tell proprietor what only I had seen
14. Found him shouting into telephone: "Yeh, big fellow. Threw bricks or something and broke my window. Want him arrested."
15. Decided to keep quiet and get out of there—fast
CLOSING SENTENCE: What would you have done?

Now look at the notes you prepared for your talk. Since the important details are already in the order in which they occurred, you have to decide only how to group related sentences for your written paragraphs. Your first paragraph will, of course, begin with the opening sentence you prepared for your talk. How many of the important details that follow are needed to make clear where the incident occurred and how you happened to see it take place? In telling what happened, the first paragraph usually gives the setting or background for the incident. What details will you have in the first paragraph of your composition?

Your second paragraph might then begin with the first detail of what you actually saw happen as the incident occurred. If your plan shows only a few more details and these are about the incident itself,

you may end this paragraph with the closing sentence you prepared for your talk. If there are other details that tell what caused the incident or how it affected you, you may simply end your second paragraph with the last important detail of the incident itself. Look again at your notes. What details in your list will you have in your second paragraph? Will you need a third paragraph in your composition?

Your third paragraph, if you need one, might begin with the first detail giving your explanation of what happened or your reaction to the incident. This final paragraph ends, of course, with the last important detail or the closing sentence prepared for your talk. Do not add anything else. What details will you have in your third paragraph?

Now mark your notes so that you will know where each paragraph begins and ends. Then write your account of the incident just as you planned to tell it in class. Use pencil and scratch paper for this first attempt—or draft—and write rapidly. You will have a chance to make changes and corrections later. Keep your classmates in mind as you write, since you may be asked to read your composition aloud to them. Try to *hear* the sentences before you put them on paper.

Once you have a first draft, you are ready for the next step— revision—in which you begin to use what you have been learning

12

about sentences. Does each sentence begin with a capital letter and end with a period, a question mark, or an exclamation mark? Does each sentence contain a subject and a verb? Is every sentence a statement? If so, can you make your sentences more interesting by changing one or two to a question or a command? Can you make your sentences clearer by using more exact modifiers or by getting rid of unnecessary words? Can you make the thought easier to follow by beginning an occasional sentence with *Then, Next, Later, Suddenly, Finally,* or some other adverb? Have you spelled every word correctly? Have you used commas where they are needed? Does every sentence say what you mean? Will that meaning be clear to the reader?

Revision is the most important step in learning to write better. It is the way in which writers—students and professionals alike—learn to express themselves in clear, forceful, interesting sentences that others can read with understanding and enjoyment. At first, it may seem mechanical—a mere correcting of careless slips in spelling and punctuation. Later, as you become acquainted with various ways in which you can use words to express your ideas, it may become more exciting—a challenge to say in every sentence and every paragraph exactly what you mean.

There are many Hollywood stories about the importance of titles, about movies that fail under one title and become box-office favorites under another. If you have done your very best in revising your first draft, you will naturally be interested in selecting a title that will make others want to read your composition. Thinking up such a title tests your ingenuity. It can be clever or amusing or have a hidden meaning that is not clear until the composition has been read. But it should be brief and not tell too much.

If you were writing about the unusual accident, you would not want a title like "The Time I Saw a Hook-and-Ladder Truck Side-swipe a Parked Car and Force It across the Sidewalk into a Store Window." Such a title is too long and tells too much. A better title would be one that merely suggests you had seen something unusual or that it had had an unexpected outcome:

I Was There	A Mysterious Mishap
The Man Was Mad	A Puzzled Proprietor

Short sentences or words beginning with the same letter often make interesting titles. So do expressions that have a familiar sound to them:

Sneak Attack	Stranger Than Fiction
Smash Hit	The Better Part of Valor
Mad Hatter	Through the Looking Glass

As you can see, a good title should be brief and should suggest more than it tells.

Now think about possible titles for the incident you have written about. Remember to keep them short—five or six words at the most. Then select one that will make the reader say to himself, "That sounds interesting. I wonder what it is about."

The final step is to copy your revised first draft in a form suitable for handing in. The first part of this lesson explained how written compositions should look. Your teacher may have added suggestions. Write as legibly as you can, keeping margins even and spacing words carefully. When you have finished, you are ready to proofread your final draft. Read it over carefully to make sure that you have not omitted anything, that you have spelled all words correctly, and that you have put in all necessary punctuation marks. If you have corrections, make them as neatly as you can.

Your teacher may ask you to read your composition to your classmates before handing it in. If so, read slowly and distinctly. Make sure that those farthest from you can hear what you say. When a classmate is reading his composition, listen carefully so that you can tell what you like about it and can ask questions about anything you do not understand.

Additional topics for Units 2-9 are suggested on pages 70 and 71.

Telling How Something Looks

Telling How Something Looks PART ONE: ORAL

There is an old Chinese saying about a picture being worth a thousand words. But a picture is not always available. And when it is not, words can be a remarkably good substitute if you have skill in telling how something looks. With words alone you can help others form an accurate mental image of something they may never have seen or noticed. Whether taking part in conversations and discussions or writing letters and reports, you will often find this skill useful.

In giving a talk about how something looks, the details you use are important; for they are the means by which a mental image is formed. The more of them you can base on personal observation, the more accurate that image is likely to be. For this reason, the best subjects for such a talk are usually places and things that are close at hand and familiar to you. You might, for example, tell about something connected with your school—the cafeteria or the biology laboratory or the bus you ride to and from school. You might enjoy telling about something at home—an attic full of strange odds and ends or your father's workshop in the basement or the outdoor fireplace you built in the back yard. You might even tell about something in the community—a favorite eating spot or movie theater, an unusual building or a new store, an interesting farm or factory, a busy airport or bus terminal.

Now think about possible subjects for your talk. Will you tell about something connected with your school, your home, the community or the neighborhood in which you live? Be sure to select some place or thing that you know well so that you can recall enough details to make an interesting talk.

Selecting suitable details for your talk is easier if you have a **point of view**. Where would a person have to stand or sit or walk to see what you are going to describe? Suppose, for example, that you are going to tell about your favorite movie theater. You might decide to tell what the interior looks like from a seat near the front. As long as that is your point of view, you would give only those details that can be seen from that one place. To include details about the popcorn machine in the lobby or the girl at the ticket window would confuse your listeners. On the other hand, you might decide to tell about approaching the elaborate entrance and walking through the enormous lobby before going into the main part of the theater itself. Then, since your point of view moves from place to place, you would give details that can be seen from each place. Now decide what the point of view will be for your talk. Will you give details that can be seen from one place or from several places?

The next step is to make a list of all the details you might use in your talk. At the top of a sheet of paper, write your point of view. Then jot down quickly all the details you think of. Be sure that each can be seen from the one or more places covered by your point of view. When you have finished, look carefully at the details in your list. Cross off any that are obvious or that nobody cares to know. For example, you need not mention that a room has four walls. Nor do you need to describe the floor or the ceiling unless there is something unusual about it. The important details are those that make the room different from other rooms. What are the important details for your subject?

In telling how something looks, you help others form a clear mental image by keeping closely related details together and by giving them in a straight line. One way of doing this is to arrange your important details in a **space order**. In telling about a basement workshop, you might start with the power tools at the left, describe the workbench in the center, and end with the paint shelves at the right. Or in telling about the exterior of a new house, you might walk around it, telling how it looks from the front, the side, the back, the other side. There are many arrangements in space—left to right, bottom to top, near to far, clockwise, and so on. Which kind you use depends, of course, on your subject and on your point of view. Try to choose a natural arrangement—one that will be easy for your classmates to follow. How will you arrange the details you have listed for your talk? When you have decided, put a figure 1 in front of the detail you will give first. Then number the rest of the details in the order in which you will give them.

The secret of telling how something looks lies in making others feel that they are at your side, looking where you look, seeing what you see. If others are to have that feeling, they must be told your original point of view—the place from which your first details could be seen. And they must be warned of any change in that point of view—any turning of head or body, any movement to a different place or position. Look at the details you will give first. Is your original point of view made clear? If not, add a few words telling what it is. Then glance through the rest of the details to make sure that you have called attention to each change in your point of view. Add words wherever necessary.

A plan for telling how something looks shows the original point of view and any changes in it. It shows, too, the arrangement of the important details. For example, if you were going to tell about the school library, your plan might look like this:

1. *As you enter and walk toward center of room*, first impression is one of light.
2. Long north wall, facing doorway, entirely of windows that extend from floor to ceiling.
3. Tables and chairs arranged to take full advantage of good natural light.
4. *At your left*, you note first a well-lighted trophy case, flanked by bookshelves along wall.
5. Above bookshelves, portraits of famous authors.
6. Near south end, two big dictionaries and a large globe on separate stands.
7. Near other end, racks for newspapers and magazines.

8. *On your right,* you see card catalogue near windows.
9. About center, a curved counter where librarian and helpers charge books in and out.
10. Behind this, a big mural in soft reds, blues, and tans.
11. Portion of "stacks"—rows of metal racks for books—visible through wide archway at south end of wall.
12. *Turning to leave library,* you observe a row of filing cases at left of large glass-paned doors.
13. Above files, several colorful prints in matching frames.
14. At right of doors, a set of low shelves.
15. On wall above them, a long bulletin board covered with notices and a display of bright-colored book jackets.

Notice that the words in italics tell what the original point of view is and call attention to each change in the point of view. Notice, too, that only the details that can be seen from each point of view are mentioned at one time. Arranging details in this way makes it easier to keep a straight line as you tell how something looks. Letting your listener know the exact point of view for each group of details helps him form a clearer mental image from your words.

In the opening sentence of the talk you will, of course, want to mention what it is you are going to tell about. For example, a talk about your school library might begin with a statement such as "One of the most pleasant places in our school is the library." Or it might begin with a question such as "Have you ever taken a good look at our school library?"

The closing sentence may be simply the last detail. If this seems too abrupt, you may decide to use a special closing sentence to round off your talk or to recall what you said in the opening sentence. For the library talk a good closing sentence might be a statement: "We are indeed fortunate to have such an attractive spot for reading or studying or just browsing." Or it might be a question: "Is it any wonder that the library is so popular?" Notice that only one sentence is used and that it does not introduce a new idea.

What opening sentence will you use for your talk? When you have decided, write it at the top of a card or a small piece of paper. Under it write the important details, keeping them in order. Underline words that show your point of view so that you will remember to warn your audience of each change in it. If you decide to use a special closing sentence, keep it short; and try to have it sum up what you said about the subject. The more carefully you prepare your notes, the more they will help you.

Practice your talk once or twice before coming to class, to make sure that you know exactly how you will phrase each sentence.

If you are called on to give your talk, stand firmly on both feet, but do not remain rigidly at attention, like a soldier. Turning your body slowly from side to side, so that you face different sections of your audience, will make you more relaxed. Glance down at your notes whenever you need to, but try to keep your head up as you are talking. Since you have planned a good talk, you will want everybody to hear what you are saying.

Telling How Something Looks PART TWO: WRITTEN

You have prepared a short talk in which you told how something looks. Now you are to prepare a written description, using the notes you made for your talk. Because your notes show what you plan to say, you can devote your attention to writing a composition that will be easy for others to read and understand.

The first problem is deciding how many paragraphs you will need in your composition. Since your notes show your original point of view and changes in it, this problem is easily solved. Simply group the details that can be seen from each point of view. If you have planned to tell what a busy airport looks like from the air and from the ground, two paragraphs might be adequate. If you have planned to tell about your favorite movie theater, you might need three paragraphs—one for the entrance, one for the lobby, one for the main part of the theater. The number of paragraphs is not important, as long as each paragraph includes the details that can be seen at one time.

When the details in your notes are in a space order, you can group related details by means of lines or brackets. The underlined words showing each point of view will help you know where each group begins. Label the first group "A" and the second group "B" and so on. Then after each letter, write a few words to show how the details in that group are related. For example, if you were writing about the library in your school, your paragraph plan might look like this:

A.
First
impression

OPENING SENTENCE: One of the most pleasant places in our school is the library.

1. *As you enter and walk toward center of room,* first impression is one of light.
2. Long north wall, facing doorway, entirely of windows that extend from floor to ceiling.
3. Tables and chairs arranged to take full advantage of good natural light.

B.
West side
of room

4. *At your left,* you note first a well-lighted trophy case, flanked by bookshelves along wall.
5. Above bookshelves, portraits of famous authors.
6. Near south end, two big dictionaries and a large globe on separate stands.
7. Near other end, racks for newspapers and magazines.

C.
East side
of room

8. *On your right,* you see card catalogue near windows.
9. About center, a curved counter where librarian and helpers charge books in and out.
10. Behind this, a big mural in soft reds, blues, and tans.
11. Portion of "stacks"—rows of metal racks for books—visible through wide archway at south end of wall.

D.
South side
of room

12. *Turning to leave library,* you observe a row of filing cases at left of large, glass-paned doors.
13. Above files, several colorful prints in matching frames.
14. At right of doors, a set of low shelves.
15. On wall above them, a long bulletin board covered with notices and a display of bright-colored book jackets.

CLOSING SENTENCE: We are indeed fortunate to have such an attractive spot for reading or studying or just browsing.

You know that a description written from this plan would have four paragraphs, one for each group of details. And you can see that the opening sentence is part of the first paragraph, while the closing sentence is part of the final paragraph. Notice that the closing sentence restates the idea expressed in the opening sentence and is more specific. By restating the idea in the closing sentence, the writer emphasizes the impression he wants to leave with the reader.

Now look at the notes you prepared for your talk. How many changes in point of view are there? What details can be seen from each point of view? Use lines or brackets to show where each group of closely related details begins and ends. Next, letter each group with an "A," a "B," and so on. Then write a few words that tell how the details in each group are related. Is the opening sentence part of the first paragraph? Is the closing sentence part of the final paragraph? Does the closing sentence emphasize the impression you want the reader to carry away? A good plan will make the writing and revising of your description much easier.

Use pencil and scratch paper for your first draft, writing your description just as you would tell it in class. Try to hear your sentences as you write them down. When you finish the first paragraph, consult your plan to be sure that you have given all the details that belong in that group. Then do the same with the second paragraph, and so on to the last one.

Next comes the revision of your first draft. Read your sentences over carefully. Does each one have a subject and a verb? Have you shown where each sentence begins and ends? Can you make any of your sentences clearer by moving a word or a phrase? You might also try to think of better modifiers for describing shape or color or size more exactly. Can you make any of your sentences more forceful by beginning with an object or by using an active verb? Perhaps you can combine a pair of related sentences by using an appositive or a participial phrase. Have you used commas  where they are needed? Are you sure of the spelling of every word? Have you used appropriate forms of verbs and pronouns? Do your sentences occasionally begin with something besides the subject? Are there any unnecessary words you can cross out?

Now read your revised sentences over rapidly. Think of what they will mean to your reader. Have you made clear what it is you are describing? Does the first paragraph tell the original point of view? Are there words in each of the other paragraphs to warn the reader of changes in point of view? Have you made clear the relationship of the sentences in each paragraph? Only by putting yourself in the place of your reader can you find weaknesses in your own writing. Revision gives you an opportunity to correct such weaknesses before others find them, too.

Thinking up a good title for something you have written is always a challenge. How much should you tell? What words should you use to make others want to read your paper? If you are describing something of great interest to many people, a simple title such as "A Modern Television Studio" is often adequate. But for subjects of less general interest, a title that arouses curiosity is more likely to attract attention. For example, instead of "Our School Library" one of the following titles might be more effective:

Adventure Depot	Where Feeds the Mind
Reader's Delight	Fact and Fancy for All
Warehouse of Wisdom	Bookworm Boardinghouse
Stop, Read, and Relax	A Bright Spot in Your Day

Now think up a good title for the description you have written. Will you tell outright what it is about? Or will you try to arouse the curiosity of the reader?

Then proofread your final draft to make sure that you have not omitted anything or made any careless slips. Have you copied any words twice? Have you left out any words or letters or punctuation marks? Have you divided words properly at the ends of lines? If there are corrections, make them neatly.

Your teacher may ask you to read your composition to your classmates before turning it in. If so, read slowly and pronounce words distinctly. Try keeping your eyes several words ahead of your voice so that you can glance up occasionally. Talk over the top of your paper, not into it. While a classmate is reading his composition, try to form a mental image from his words. Be ready to ask questions about anything that is not clear to you and to suggest ways in which his composition might be improved.

Telling About Interesting People

Telling about Interesting People PART ONE: ORAL

Unless you happen to be a hermit living a solitary life in a cave, you are very likely more interested in other human beings than you are in anything else in the world. Naturally you are interested in many famous personalities that you have become acquainted with through the movies, the newspapers, the radio, and television. But you are also very much interested in certain individuals that most of the world probably never heard of and never will—your friends, members of your family, people living in your town or neighborhood.

What interesting person could you choose to tell your classmates about in an oral report? You can forget about the famous folks (who get too much attention anyway) and think about the interesting people you know personally. An aunt who writes poetry or paints in her spare time, a bus driver who talks an ear off every customer, a little sister who stomps around in high heels and plays "movie star," a policeman who fancies himself a Sherlock Holmes—any such person would make an interesting subject.

In the few minutes you will have for your talk, you cannot, of course, tell everything you know about such a person. You must limit yourself to the two or three points that you think would be most interesting to your classmates. For example, you might describe how the person looks, what work he does, and what quality about him most impresses you. You might describe the kind of person he used to be and the kind of person he is now. Or you might prefer to tell a little about his appearance and a great deal about his accomplishments. Whatever you decide, plan to include in your talk an incident in which the person actually talks. By quoting his own words, you will make him seem more real.

When you have decided what points you will cover in your talk, make a list of details, arranging them in separate groups in a logical order. For example, if you were going to tell about a relative of yours —an Uncle Elmer who runs a general store in a small town—your list might look like this:

Appearance —
1. Short, tubby, jolly—about 55 years old
2. Few strands of dark hair plastered across shiny scalp
3. Plain but pleasant face, gold-rimmed spectacles
4. Has two pairs of glasses, one kept at home
5. Low, quiet voice and hearty laugh

Work —
1. Sells everything—groceries, meats, hardware, dry goods, etc.
2. Long hours—7:30 A.M. to 10:30 P.M.
3. Always wears white wrap-around store apron
4. Never too busy to help customers with their problems
5. Creates good will by letting everyone use store as meeting place, debate hall
6. (Incident showing his way of breaking up angry argument)

Outstanding quality —
1. Always generous
2. Lends money to anyone with hard-luck story
3. Can't bear to enforce credit rules
4. Sees that needy customers get 13 in every dozen, 18 ounces in every pound
5. Keeps prices as low as he can—sometimes lower

The next two steps are important. First, check over your list to make sure there are no unnecessary items, duplications, or other errors. Second, think of a main heading for each group that will show your listeners how the details in the group are related. For example:

Though as a baby my Uncle Elmer won first prize in a "pretty baby" contest, he is now quite ordinary in appearance.

    A. Short, tubby, jolly—about 55 years old

    B. Few strands of dark hair plastered across shiny scalp

    C. Plain but pleasant face, gold-rimmed spectacles

    D. Low, quiet voice and hearty laugh

    E. Always wears white wrap-around store apron

He owns and manages the only store in a very small town.

    A. Sells everything—groceries, meats, hardware, dry goods, etc.

    B. Long hours—7:30 A.M. to 10:30 P.M.

    C. Creates good will by letting everyone use store as meeting place, debate hall

    D. (Incident showing his way of breaking up angry argument)

Uncle Elmer is the most generous person I know.

    A. Lends money to anyone with hard-luck story

    B. Can't bear to enforce credit rules

    C. Sees that needy customers get 13 in every dozen, 18 ounces in every pound

    D. Keeps prices as low as he can—sometimes lower

Notice that several items in the list on page 24 have been changed. Item 4 of the first group has been omitted from the plan, since it has nothing to do with Elmer's appearance. Item 3 of the second group has been shifted to the first group, since it is a detail of Elmer's appearance rather than of his work. And Item 1 of the third group has been included in the main heading for the group.

Now look at the list of details for your talk, checking it carefully to make sure that you have included no unnecessary items and that each item is in the right group. Make sure that you have included also an incident involving a conversation. Then write out a plan for your talk. What will you use for the main heading for each group of details?

There is no need for a special opening sentence in a talk like this. But you may want to use a special closing sentence to sum up your feeling about the person. For example: "I wish there were enough Uncle Elmers to go around, so that every town could have one." If you decide to use such a sentence, write it at the end of your plan.

Copy your final plan on a card or small piece of paper, so that your notes will be inconspicuous and easy to handle as you speak. Then practice your talk several times before you go to class. Try to talk in a natural, conversational tone. Remember that you are not making a great, important speech. You are merely telling a group of friends about an interesting person you would like them to know as you do. Since you have included a conversation in your talk, try various ways of saying the sentences you will be quoting.

Telling about Interesting People PART TWO: WRITTEN

You have prepared a talk about some interesting person you know. Now you are to write a composition about that person, using the notes you made for your talk.

First you must think about the number of paragraphs you will use. In the composition assignments you have had so far, you have used a separate paragraph for each group of related details in your plan. In this assignment the problem is somewhat different, since you were asked to include some conversation in your description. If you are quoting only one remark made by your subject, that remark will be a part of the paragraph you make from the group of details in which it appears. But if you are using **dialogue**—conversation between two or more persons—you will need to make a separate paragraph for what each person says at one time. Thus a single item in a group of details in your plan might take several paragraphs.

Look at the plan for the talk about Uncle Elmer, on page 24. If you were writing a composition from this plan, the first group of details, describing Uncle Elmer's appearance, and the last group of details, describing his generosity, would be single paragraphs in your composition. But notice the second group of details, which describe the way Uncle Elmer runs his store. The last item in the group is an incident involving conversation. Remembering that a separate paragraph is needed for what each person in a dialogue says at one time, you might write about the incident like this:

> One night last summer an argument in the back of the store was growing louder and angrier by the minute. Uncle Elmer called back to the group, "Say, boys, why don't you buy yourselves a bottle of pop? Maybe it'll cool you off a bit."

26

"O.K., Elmer, I get the idea," said Joe Adams, walking away from the group.

Bill Phelps, who was not so easily persuaded, protested, "Now look here, Elmer, let us finish this thing."

Uncle Elmer was quiet for a minute. Then looking squarely at him, he said, "Good night, Bill. Come in again tomorrow."

Big, 200-pound Bill Phelps meekly left the store without another word, and the other fellows sat down, looking a little shamefaced. Because everyone likes and respects Uncle Elmer, he has little trouble keeping his "guests" in line.

Notice that each paragraph in the dialogue includes not only the exact words that were said, but also other words explaining who said them and under what circumstances. Notice also that *said* is not the only word used to indicate that someone talks. *Called* and *protested* are used in place of *said* with two of the speeches.

Now write the first draft of your composition, following your plan carefully. Use the main heading of each group of details as a topic sentence for the paragraph about these details. The topic sentences tell your reader how the details are related. And in the paragraphs after the first, the topic sentences warn your reader when you move from one group of details to another. You do not need topic sentences in the dialogue paragraphs, since the details in these follow a natural time order. Be sure to use a separate paragraph for the words each speaker says at one time, as in the example shown on pages 26 and 27.

When you have finished writing your first draft, proofread it carefully. Then improve your sentences wherever you can—using more exact words, varying the order of the words, combining related sentences to make better ones. Correct any errors in spelling and punctuation. If necessary, review the punctuation lesson in this Unit before you check the punctuation of your direct quotations.

You can use the name of the person you are telling about as the title of your composition—for example, Uncle Elmer, David Nelson, Dr. Alan Kent. But if you want to experiment a bit with titles, you may be able to think up one that will be more likely to catch the reader's attention. For example, the composition on Uncle Elmer might have any one of the following titles:

The Unofficial Mayor of Elmwood	Angel in a White Apron
Kindness, Incorporated	Rich Little Poor Man
Big Frog in a Little Puddle	A Store of Wisdom

What title will you use for your composition?

Now you are ready to make the final copy of your composition. Write down your title, and copy your first draft, paying careful attention to all the changes and corrections you have made. Keep margins even, and space your words so that your writing will be easy to read. Use equal indentions for the first words of all the paragraphs, including those in the dialogue. When you have finished copying, give your composition a final proofreading, so that you can catch any errors you may have made. Make corrections as neatly as you can, since this is the paper you are going to hand in.

Practice reading your composition aloud before you come to class. If you are called on to read it to your classmates, remember to change your voice slightly to indicate a change in speaker and to make your quoted remarks sound as natural as possible. Read slowly and distinctly, and be sure that everyone can hear you.

Listen carefully to your classmates as they read their compositions. You will want to be able to tell what you like about each composition you hear and what you think might be improved in each.

Telling How Something Is Made Or Done

Telling How Something Is Made or Done   PART ONE: ORAL

You know that this page is made of paper. Could you explain to your classmates how the paper was made from trees or how these words were printed on it? If so, your classmates would probably pay close attention; for almost everyone is interested in knowing how something is made or done. Across the length and breadth of our land millions of people are busily engaged in producing things we need and want. You may have actually seen some of these things being manufactured. You may have learned about others at home or in school. You may have read about processes that have to do with your interest in hobbies and sports—how coins are minted, how radar operates, how fancy diving is judged. Because people are usually curious about such things, you will find them interested in a simple explanation that makes clear the steps in a process you know about.

For this composition assignment you are to prepare a talk in which you explain to your classmates how something is made or done. You might, for example, tell how wallpaper or pottery or camera film is made. Or you might tell how coal is mined, how milk reaches our homes, or how vegetables are prepared for shipping to market. If you choose a process that you already know about or have actually seen carried out, you will have little difficulty in remembering the important steps in it. But try to choose a subject that really interests you, even if it means asking questions or looking up details that you are not sure about. What will you tell about?

When you have decided on a subject, think about it carefully. What details do you know about the process? What are the important steps in it? What interesting facts do you know about it? As you are thinking, jot down the details that come to your mind. Write them down quickly and briefly as they occur to you, so that you do not forget any of them.

Now look carefully at the list of details you made for your talk. Think about what you are going to say, and cross off any details that might distract your classmates or lead them away from your subject. Then put a number 1 in front of the detail that occurs first. Number the remaining details in the exact order in which they are to be used.

For example, if you were going to tell how major-league baseballs are made, your list of details might look like this:

~~Like to take automobile trips with family~~
~~One summer went to Yellowstone National Park~~
~~Last summer went to New England~~
~~Visited large sporting-goods factory~~
~~Saw how major-league baseballs are made~~
1. Core, or center, made of cork and rubber
2. Piece of cork composition compressed to size of a marble
3. Two small rubber cups fitted over cork
4. Whole thing then enclosed in molded rubber casing
6. Next, four layers of yarn wound over this core
8. First winding 121 yards of one kind of gray yarn
9. Second winding 45 yards of another kind of gray yarn
10. Third winding 53 yards of a cream-colored yarn
11. Fourth winding 150 yards of white cotton yarn
12. Ball then dipped in rubber cement to hold windings in place
13. Covers made of hides from carefully selected horses
~~Hides of ordinary dray horses likely to be scarred or cut~~
~~Shame the way some people treat horses~~
14. Two shaped pieces of damp horsehide stretched over yarn
15. Edges sewed together by hand, using 108 stitches
16. Leather shrinks as it dries, making smooth, tight-fitting cover
17. When dry, cover stamped with blue Reach label for American League or black Spalding label for National League
18. All major-league baseballs made in same factory and in same way

7. Automatic machines used in winding yarn to keep tension constant

5. Famous "cushioned cork center" used for over 20 years

~~Baseball a great game to play and to watch~~

~~Like it best of all sports~~

Notice that nine details have been crossed off. They are not needed to tell how a baseball is made. The first five are about automobile trips. The two near the middle are concerned with cruelty to animals. The last two introduce a new topic—baseball as a sport. Eliminating distracting details enables a speaker to keep to his subject.

Notice, too, that the details are numbered to show the order in which they are to be used. The actual steps in making a baseball are in the order of their occurrence. Facts closely related to these steps—such as details 13, 18, 7, and 5—are numbered to show their relationship to the other details. A good rule is to cross off any detail that cannot be grouped with others.

In telling how something is made or done, you might begin with a statement of the main steps in the process. Or you might explain briefly how you happen to know about it. Or you might use a question to rouse the listener's interest or curiosity. For example, the opening sentence of the baseball talk might be: "There are three important steps in the making of baseballs for major-league teams: forming the center, winding the yarn, and putting on the cover." Or it might be: "On a trip through a large sporting-goods factory last summer I learned how major-league baseballs are made." Or it might be: "Did you know that the baseballs used by both major leagues are exactly alike?" But notice that only one sentence is used.

A special closing sentence is seldom needed in telling how something is made or done. You simply end with the last detail. For example: "I was certainly surprised to discover that all major-league baseballs are made in the same factory and in exactly the same way."

How will you begin your talk? As soon as you have decided on a good opening sentence, write it at the top of a card or a piece of paper. Under it write your plan, listing the details in the order in which you numbered them.

Unit 5   Telling How Something Is Made or Done   31

These are the notes for your talk. Have them in your hand as you practice, glancing at them whenever you are in doubt about what comes next. If you are asked to give your talk, stand up and wait for your classmates to become quiet. Then take a deep breath and begin. Speak slowly and clearly. Hold your head up so that all can hear.

One idea at a time

Have you ever hunted for paper clips in a box that also contained rubber bands, thumb tacks, pencil stubs, and old erasers? If you have, you know that it is much easier to find the paper clips when they are in a box by themselves. Likewise, it is easier for a reader to understand details when they are grouped with others of the same kind. Just as an orderly desk will have one place for paper clips, another for rubber bands, still another for thumb tacks, so an orderly written composition will have a separate paragraph for each group of closely related details.

Paragraphs, like boxes, are of different sizes, depending on what goes into them. Some may be as short as one sentence. A few may be as long as twenty or more sentences. The great majority are neither that short nor that long. But however much paragraphs may vary in length, the reader expects each one to be concerned with a single idea. Nothing is more annoying to a reader than having to sort out details that have to do with several ideas.

Whenever you express ideas in writing that you want others to read and understand, it is up to you, the writer, to be sure that the sentences in each paragraph are closely related and have to do with one idea, one part of your subject. By keeping together all the details that have to do with that idea, you make it easier for the reader to understand that part of your subject before he goes on to the next. By taking up one idea at a time, you make it easier for him to understand your subject as a whole.

Telling How Something Is Made or Done PART TWO: WRITTEN

You have prepared an oral report in which you explained how something is made or done. Now you are to prepare a written report on the same subject, using the notes you made for your talk. Since these notes show how you planned to begin and what you planned to say, you can concentrate on the problems of writing a report.

First comes the problem of deciding how many paragraphs you will need. This is done by consulting your notes to see how many groups of closely related details there are. You will probably find that each group has to do with one important part or phase of your subject. By telling about each group of details in a separate paragraph, you will help the reader know the plan of your report.

It is easy to organize paragraphs when the details are arranged in the order of their occurrence. You need only mark each group with a line or bracket. You will find it helpful also to label the first group "A," the second group "B," and so on, and tell in a few words how the details in each group are related. For example, if you were preparing a written report about the making of major-league baseballs, your plan might look like this:

	OPENING SENTENCE: On a trip through a large sporting-goods factory last summer I learned how major-league baseballs are made.
A. Forming the center	1. Core, or center, made of cork and rubber
	2. Piece of cork composition compressed to size of a marble
	3. Two small rubber cups fitted over cork
	4. Whole thing then enclosed in molded rubber casing
	5. This the famous "cushioned cork center" used for over 20 years

B.
Winding
the yarn
{
6. Next, four layers of yarn wound over this core
7. Automatic machines used in winding yarn to keep tension constant
8. First winding 121 yards of one kind of gray yarn
9. Second winding 45 yards of another kind of gray yarn
10. Third winding 53 yards of a cream-colored yarn
11. Fourth winding 150 yards of white cotton yarn
12. Ball then dipped in rubber cement to hold windings in place

C.
Putting on
the cover
{
13. Covers made of hides from carefully selected horses
14. Two shaped pieces of damp horsehide stretched over yarn
15. Edges sewed together by hand, using 108 stitches
16. Leather shrinks as it dries, making smooth, tight-fitting cover
17. When dry, cover stamped with blue Reach label for American League or black Spalding label for National League

CLOSING SENTENCE: I was certainly surprised to discover that all major-league baseballs are made in the same factory and in exactly the same way.

You can see that this plan is for a report that is to have three paragraphs, one for each of the important steps in making a baseball. Notice that the opening sentence is part of the first paragraph. Notice that the closing sentence is part of the final paragraph. Separate paragraphs for the introduction and the conclusion are rarely used in a short written report.

Now look at the notes you prepared for your talk. How many groups of closely related details are there? Use lines or brackets to show where each group begins and ends. Next, letter each group with an "A," a "B," and so on. Then write a few words to show how the details in each group are related. Is the opening sentence part of the first paragraph? Is the closing sentence part of the final paragraph? This is to be the plan for your report. A little care in preparing it will make the writing and revising easier for you.

When your plan is ready, write your explanation just as you planned to tell it in class. Use pencil and scratch paper for this first draft, and write rapidly to get your ideas down on paper. Follow your plan so that each paragraph is made up of closely related details.

The next problem is revising your first draft to make your written sentences clear, forceful, and interesting to read. Does each sentence have a subject and a verb? Have you shown clearly where each sentence begins and ends? Do most of your sentences begin with the subject? If so, can you occasionally begin with the verb or an adverb or a preposition to break the monotony of subject-verb, subject-verb, subject-verb? Are there any sentences that can be made more forceful by beginning with an object? Are you sure of the spelling of every word? Have you used commas wherever necessary—and only where needed? Do your sentences say exactly what you mean?

Revision is more than merely correcting mistakes. It is more, even, than improving sentences. Revision is the time for thinking about what you have written, for seeing that you have carried out your plan, for being sure that you have expressed your ideas clearly. Does each paragraph explain one part of the process? Is it clear what that part is? Have you made clear the relationship of the details in each group? Do you need words like *first, next, then, finally*—or phrases like *in the beginning, before long, at last*—to show how the paragraphs are related? Always consider the reader. Keep asking yourself, "Have I made my meaning clear?" Only when you can answer Yes, are you through revising your first draft.

A good title, like a good advertising slogan, attracts attention. Its function is to make others want to read what you have written, and usually it must do this in not more than half a dozen words. When you are sure that the subject is of sufficient interest to make others want to read your report, you may use a simple, straightforward title such as "How Major-League Baseballs Are Made." When you are not sure, it is better to use a title that arouses interest or curiosity by merely suggesting your subject:

Birth of a Baseball	Flying Horsehide
Slugger's Delight	Undercover Information
Baseball Yarn	Homer Bound

Notice that such titles are brief and do not tell the reader too much.

When you have decided on a suitable title, you are ready to prepare your final draft. Write your title on the first line. Under it copy your revised first draft as legibly as you can. Then proofread your final draft to make sure that you have not omitted anything or made any careless slips. If there are corrections, make them neatly.

Your teacher may ask you to read your report to your classmates before handing it in. If so, read slowly and pronounce words distinctly. Keep your paper down and your head up. Try to talk over the top of your paper so that everyone can hear. When a classmate is reading his report, listen carefully so that you can tell what you like about it and can ask questions about anything you do not understand.

Telling What Something Means

Telling What Something Means PART ONE: ORAL

If we used only "concrete" words—like *policeman* and *lake* and *newspaper*—we would have little trouble in communicating our thoughts. Because concrete words are names of people, places, and objects—persons and things that actually exist—they have much the same general meaning to everyone who knows them. Even if we use a concrete word that is new to our listeners—say *duralumin* or *jabot* or *creese*—we can always define it by describing in a few words the thing it names.

It is when we use "abstract" words—like *loyalty, friendship, wisdom, art, success, socialism, beauty, culture, Americanism*—that we run into difficulty in making our thoughts clear to others. Since abstract words are names of ideas, which exist only in our minds, they rarely have the same meaning to people who use them. To you the word *sophistication* has one meaning; to the boy at your left it has another; to the girl at your right it has still another. To Selina Peake, the heroine of *So Big*, there was "beauty" in a field of cabbage plants. To the owners of the field there was not. The word *beauty* meant one thing to Selina, another to the farmers of the community. It means still another to you.

In using abstract words, you may not be clearly understood unless you make clear what the words mean to you by giving specific examples of several kinds. For instance, in explaining the word *success*, you might give examples of what you consider to be success in a career, in a hobby, in financial matters, in dealings with friends and family, and so on.

For your assignment in this Unit you are to prepare an oral composition in which you tell what an abstract word or expression means to you. If you think over the conversations you have had with your friends recently, you can probably recall a number of abstract terms that were used. You may have discussed *school spirit*, for example, or *patriotism, freedom of speech, the American way of life, popularity, a sense of humor, tolerance, fair play, selfishness, true generosity*, or *a sense of responsibility*. Any abstract term that names an idea in which you and your friends are interested would make a good subject for your talk. What will your subject be?

Once you have decided on a term to explain, make a list of specific examples that illustrate what the term means to you. If, for instance, you were planning to explain the meaning of *a sense of responsibility*, your list might look like this:

1. Doing home chores without being nagged
2. Obeying family rules
3. Preparing class assignments
4. Obeying school laws
5. Being careful of things borrowed from others
6. Respecting community laws
7. Not defacing school books or wasting school supplies
8. Getting to meals without being called
9. Arriving at classes on time
10. Living up to agreements made with parents
11. Fulfilling promises made to friends and others
12. Observing traffic regulations on highway
13. Being on time for appointments, meetings, rehearsals
14. Assuming share of work for clubs, committees, school paper
15. Being careful of public property

Though this list includes enough examples for a talk, the helter-skelter order in which they are listed would probably be annoying or confusing to your listeners. The list lacks organization.

By organizing the examples into related groups and arranging the groups in a logical order, you might work out a plan that looks like this:

First, doing the work expected of you—without prompting
- A. Chores at home
- B. Assignments for classes
- C. Duties assigned by clubs, committee chairmen, etc.

Second, observing regulations
- A. At home
- B. At school
- C. In the community
- D. On the highway

Third, taking good care of property
- A. Own
- B. Borrowed
- C. School
- D. Public

Fourth, being punctual
- A. For meals at home
- B. For classes at school
- C. For appointments, rehearsals, meetings

Fifth, keeping your word
- A. Living up to agreements made with parents
- B. Carrying out promises made to friends and others

This plan shows that there are five groups of related examples, each group illustrating one of the things that reveal a sense of responsibility. Since each group is introduced by a main heading that shows how the examples in that group are related, the wording of many items in the list has been shortened. Notice the italicized words *First, Second, Third,* and so on. They help your listeners know when you are moving from one group of examples to another.

Now go over the list of details you made for your talk, and decide how many groups of related examples you will have in your plan. Write a main heading for each group to show how the examples are related. Then arrange the groups in the order that you think will be most convincing to your classmates. Make sure that your main headings include words that will help your listeners know when you are beginning a new group of examples.

What will be a good opening sentence for your talk? You might use a question: "Have you ever thought seriously about what it means to have a sense of responsibility?" Or you might open with a statement: "To me a sense of responsibility is shown by five actions that speak louder than words." When you have decided how you will begin your talk, write your opening sentence at the top of your plan.

Do you need a special closing sentence to round off your talk? If you do, add the sentence to your plan. If not, you will simply end your talk with your last example.

Copy your plan on a card or small piece of paper so that you can keep your notes in your hand as you practice your talk and as you give it. If the main headings and details in your plan are as brief as those in the plan on page 39, it is important to practice your talk two or three times so that you will know exactly how to word your sentences.

If you are called on to give your talk in class, speak as clearly and distinctly as you can. Try to look at your classmates as you talk, not at the floor or ceiling. By standing with your feet slightly apart and your weight evenly balanced, you will have good, comfortable posture. You might pause and turn slightly at the beginning of each new group of details, to help your audience become aware of each change of thought in your plan. Do not let your voice trail off at the ends of sentences. Try not to look and sound as if you were in a hurry to get back to your desk.

Telling What Something Means PART TWO: WRITTEN

You have prepared an oral composition in which you told what something means. Now you are to prepare a written composition, using the notes you made for your talk.

You will have as many paragraphs in your composition as you have groups of related examples in your plan. The items listed in each group are the details you will use for each paragraph. And since the main headings tell how the items in each group are related, they will become the topic sentences that tell what each paragraph is about.

In changing the main headings to topic sentences, try to include words that will help the reader know how the paragraphs are related to one another. For example, in a composition written from the plan on page 39, the topic sentences might be:

40

First of all, having a sense of responsibility means doing—without prompting—the work expected of you.

Second, a person with a sense of responsibility does his best to observe regulations, wherever he is.

A third sign of responsibility is respect for property—your own and that of others.

Fourth, you show a sense of responsibility by being punctual.

Finally, a responsible person always tries to keep his word.

The words *First, Second, third, Fourth,* and *Finally* link the paragraphs together and make it easy for readers to follow the thought in moving from one group of details to another. Now write the topic sentences for the paragraphs in your composition. What words will you use to show how the paragraphs are related?

As soon as you have topic sentences for your paragraphs, you are ready to start writing the first draft of your composition. Follow your plan closely. Write in pencil, and leave enough space between lines so that you will have room to make revisions. If you have a special opening sentence, remember to make it part of your first paragraph. Then write your topic sentence and, after it, one or two sentences about each of the details in the first group of your plan. Do the same for each of the remaining groups. When you come to your closing sentence, make it part of your last paragraph.

Now reread your first draft carefully to see if you have made your meaning clear. Do your topic sentences tell what each paragraph is about? Have you included words that let the reader know how the paragraphs are related to one another? Check the spelling of all words you know to be your personal demons. Make sure that any appositives, participial phrases, and adjective clauses you have used are punctuated correctly. Can you make several of your sentences more effective by combining them? Can you avoid subject-verb, subject-verb monotony by beginning an occasional sentence with an adverb, a preposition, or an object? Do not stop revising until your sentences are as good as you can make them.

Though it is satisfactory to use the term you are explaining as the title for your composition, you may want to use instead a title that will arouse curiosity or attract attention. If your opening sentence is a statement, you might use a question for your title. For example:

What Does Good Sportsmanship Mean?
Is Beauty More than Skin Deep?
What Is a Sense of Responsibility?

If your opening sentence is a question, you might use a title that suggests—rather than tells—what your composition is about:

Opponents Are People, Too
Beauty Is Where You Find It
By What We Do

What title will you use for your composition? After you have decided, copy your revised first draft neatly in ink. Then proofread your paper to catch any mistakes you may have made in copying.

You may be called on to read your composition in class. To keep from reading too rapidly, pause briefly between sentences. Listen attentively while others are reading. Your classmates will be interested in any suggestions you can make for improving their work.

Expressing an Opinion

Expressing an Opinion PART ONE: ORAL

Expressing opinions is an old American custom. Like most of your friends, you probably express many opinions during the course of the day—on subjects ranging from the breakfast food to the President's latest speech.

Many of these opinions go unquestioned. If you tell your mother the cherry pie is excellent, she is not likely to ask why you think so. But when you express an opinion on a controversial subject, you should have good reasons in mind to back up that opinion. If you say to someone from another school, "In my opinion, our basketball team will be the best in the league this year," he is likely to ask why you think so. An "Oh, just because," or something equally vague, will not keep him from considering your opinion worthless. But if you tell him some facts about veteran players, promising newcomers, the new coach's record, and the sad plight of other teams in the league, he will know that you have valid reasons for making the statement. Even though he may not agree with you, he can respect your opinion. An opinion is not a "hunch," or a prejudice, or a bit of wishful thinking. Behind any opinion that is valid there are good reasons that you can use to explain why you made up your mind as you did.

As you think about possible subjects for a talk in which you express an opinion, you will soon realize that you have some sort of opinion about every person, every event, every idea, everything you have come in contact with or heard about. What is your opinion of swimming as a sport? What do you think about getting an allowance? What opinions have you formed about gardening, opera, Fords, card games, open-book examinations, television, blue jeans? Try to choose a subject that you think will be of interest to your classmates. But do not avoid a subject just because you think they will not agree with your opinion. Whether they nod approvingly or show signs of wanting to argue as you speak will not matter. What will matter is that you give them an opinion they can understand and respect because of the reasons you use to explain it. What of your many opinions will you tell the class about?

What reasons can you give to back up the opinion you are going to discuss? Try to think of every fact that influenced you in forming your opinion. List your reasons as you think of them. Remember that the details in this list are completely personal. They should, of course, include some definite facts, but you will report these facts as they affect you. If you were going to tell why you dislike shopping, for example, you might list the following reasons:

1. Noisy, rude, jostling crowds
2. Budget limitations
3. Clerks sometimes unwilling to wait on customers
4. Insincerity of many clerks
5. Weather often unpleasant
6. Temptation to buy things other than intended purchases
7. Overall fatigue after a few hours of shopping
8. Parents' approval to be considered
9. False sales-talk about inferior merchandise
10. Overdoses of flattery as I try on clothes
11. Conflict between what I like best and what would be most practical
12. Clerks' lack of information about merchandise
13. Loss of interest when clerk finds sale is to be small
14. Transportation difficulties in crowded shopping areas
15. Clerks' haughty attitude toward clothes I'm wearing
16. Great need for more shop-by-phone services

Your own list of details, like this list, may be somewhat unorganized. You will want to put the details into related groups so that you can present your reasons in a logical order. If you were going to give the talk on shopping, you might first ask yourself, "What are my main reasons for disliking shopping?" Then, as you studied the list, you would find that several of the details are concerned with personal discomforts—jostling crowds, unpleasant weather, and so on. Some of the other details are concerned with annoying habits of clerks. And most of the remaining details deal with the problems of deciding what to buy. If you put the related details into these three groups, your plan might look like this:

For one thing, there are too many personal discomforts.
    A. Noisy, rude, jostling crowds
    B. Weather often unpleasant
    C. Transportation difficulties in crowded shopping areas
    D. Overall fatigue after a few hours of shopping
Furthermore, I always have trouble deciding what to buy.
    A. Budget limitations
    B. Parents' approval to be considered
    C. Temptation to buy things other than intended purchases
    D. Conflict between what I like best and what would be most practical
Finally, clerks can sometimes be very annoying.
    A. Lack of information about merchandise
    B. Unwillingness to wait on customers
    C. False sales-talk about inferior merchandise
    D. Overdoses of flattery as I try on clothes
    E. Haughty attitude toward clothes I'm wearing
    F. Loss of interest if sale is to be small

Notice that each group has a main heading that tells how the details in that group are related. Notice, too, the italicized words that show the relationship of the groups to one another. Two of the details in the list do not appear in the plan: Item 4 was omitted because the same idea is covered by two other details, the ones concerned with flattery and sales-talk. And Item 16 was omitted because it is not actually a reason why shopping is so distasteful, but a suggestion for eliminating shopping.

Now study your list of details. How are the various reasons related to one another? Arrange them in groups, and then write a main heading at the top of each group to explain the relationship. Experiment with the order of your groups and with the order of the details within each group. Arrange them in the order that you think will be most effective in your talk, but try to place the most important reasons last, so that you can give the effect of building up your case as you go along.

What opening sentence will you use for your talk? You might begin by simply stating your opinion: "Shopping, in my opinion, is a thoroughly unpleasant task." Or you might use exaggeration to emphasize your feeling and to arouse the interest of your audience: "If I were given a choice of enduring twenty lashes, going without dessert for six months, or spending an afternoon shopping, I wouldn't choose shopping." When you have decided how you will begin your talk, write your opening sentence at the top of your plan.

You will not want to end your talk with the last detail in your plan, as you have done in some previous compositions. One of the best ways to round off a talk of this kind is to restate your opinion, since that is the thought you want to leave with your audience. Decide what your closing sentence will be, and write it at the bottom of your plan. Then give your plan a final check to see if it can be improved.

Copy your plan on a card or small piece of paper. Write as neatly as possible, but do not write too small in your effort to save space. You want to be able to follow your notes easily as you speak, without having to stop to decipher your handwriting. Practice your talk once or twice so that you will be familiar with your notes.

Expressing an Opinion PART TWO: WRITTEN

You have prepared an oral composition in which you expressed an opinion and gave reasons to support it. Now you are to prepare a written composition, using the notes you made for your talk. Because you have already done the necessary planning, you can concentrate here on expressing your ideas in writing.

The first step is to look over your plan to see how many paragraphs your composition will have. As you know, each group of related details will be explained in a separate paragraph. And the main heading of each group becomes the topic sentence that tells what the paragraph is about.

How many paragraphs will you have in your composition? If you have a special opening sentence, remember to make it part of your first paragraph. And make your special closing sentence a part of your last paragraph.

Now write the first draft of your composition, using pencil and scratch paper, so that you can make changes easily. Write just as though you were explaining your opinion and your reasons to your friends—which is exactly what you will be doing if you are called on to read your composition in class. You can be as informal and chatty as you like; for this composition, remember, comes under the heading of "strictly personal."

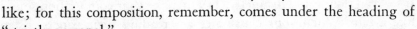

The next step is to revise your first draft. Read through the paragraphs slowly and critically. Do the topic sentences explain how the details in each paragraph are related? Can you add a word or a phrase to show the reader how the second paragraph is related to the first? Have you used exact adjectives and avoided unnecessary words? Are the modifying words, phrases, and clauses placed so that they clearly modify the right words? Look for sentences that can be combined to express more effectively and exactly the meaning you had in mind. Check the punctuation and the spelling, referring to the dictionary when in doubt about a word. Try not to be satisfied with your first draft until you have made each sentence and each paragraph as good as is possible.

Now you are ready to think of a title for your composition. You might use a title that simply states your opinion:

I Dislike Shopping   I Hate Cats
Football Is a Wonderful Sport   Family Reunions Are Fun

Or you might try to think up a title that would be more likely to catch your reader's interest—one that states your opinion in an unusual way or that merely hints at what your opinion is. For example, compare these titles with those at the bottom of the preceding page:

Pity the Poor Shopper!	Cats? Phooey!
Bone-Crushing Bargain Hunters	Why Is a Cat?
Gridiron Glamor	Shaking the Family Tree
Don't Block That Kick!	Relatives Are Relatively Nice

What title will you use for your composition? Write the one you decide on at the top of your paper.

Then copy your first draft carefully. Keep the margins even, and indent all paragraphs equally. Write as legibly as you can, leaving spaces between words. When you have finished, proofread your work, making sure no new errors have appeared. If there are corrections, make them neatly.

Your teacher may ask you to read your composition to the class. If so, read slowly and distinctly. Try to make your composition sound like a talk. When your classmates are reading their papers, listen thoughtfully so that you will be ready to make helpful criticisms.

Expressing a Preference

Unit 8

Expressing a Preference PART ONE: ORAL

Which do you like better—a circus or a carnival? If you were offered two summer jobs at the same pay—one indoor work, the other outdoor—which would you take? Which subject would you sign up for —biology or chemistry? Would you rather spend your time listening to radio programs or watching television? Which would you choose for making a long pleasure trip—train or automobile? In answering questions of this sort, you express a preference. How convincing your answer is to others often depends on the reasons you give to explain your preference.

As you can see, each of the questions involves making a choice between two things of the same kind. If that choice is to be based on facts rather than on feelings alone, it is necessary to compare the two things, considering carefully the differences between them, weighing the advantages of one against the advantages of the other. A preference arrived at in this way can be explained by giving the important points of comparison.

For this assignment you are to prepare an oral report in which you express a preference and give reasons for your choice. The questions in the first paragraph should start you thinking about possible subjects that involve choosing between two similar things—sports, hobbies, clothes, automobiles, vacations, careers, and so on. Whenever you feel that some persons might prefer one choice and some another, you probably have a good subject. If it interests you personally, you will have no difficulty thinking of enough points of comparison to make it interesting to your classmates. What subject will you use?

Now think carefully about your subject. What are the points of difference? One way of keeping them in order is to list the advantages of each of the two things you are comparing. Jot them down as they come to your mind, keeping them in separate groups. Then go over your list. Are there any items that are not really points of difference? Are there duplications—two items covering one advantage? Is there any item expressed as a disadvantage that could be put in the other group as an advantage? For example, if you were explaining your preference for making a long pleasure trip by car, your list might look like this:

By car—
  Costs less if several share expenses
  Can make side trips, see more scenery
  No worry about reservations, schedules, transfers
  Traffic problems are nuisance
  Can carry baggage more conveniently
  Can stop overnight at motels —with car handy
  No worry about getting baggage to hotel
  Can eat in different places or buy food to take along
  Can drive right up to destination
  No porters to tip
  Can meet interesting people on way
By train—
  Usually faster
  Meals no problem —diner or club car
  Interesting people to talk to
  Can stand up, stretch, wander about
  Can sleep in comfort —adjustable seats or Pullman
  No worry about missing way, flat tires, gas, etc.
  No worry about traffic problems

Notice that the last item in the first group and the third in the second group have been crossed out. Neither of these items is a point of difference. The seventh item in the first group has also been crossed out because it merely duplicates the fifth item. And the fourth item in the first group has been crossed out because it is a disadvantage. The idea has been rephrased as an advantage and added to the second group. In expressing a preference, you will usually find it easier to word the points of difference as advantages.

Notice, too, that the advantages of traveling by car are all in one group, while the advantages of traveling by train are in another group. The arrangement of ideas in related groups is called a **logical order**. A logical order is often used for details that cannot be arranged in a time order or a space order.

When you have the advantages on your list clearly separated into logical groups, look at the items in each group. Which item will you mention first? Which will you mention next and next and so on to the last—and most important—one? Then number the items in each group according to the order in which you plan to give them.

The next step, once your two groups of advantages are complete and numbered, is to think of a sentence for each group to show your listeners how the details are related. In the talk expressing a choice between a train trip and a car trip, you would first discuss the advantages of going by train, since it is usually most effective to end with the advantages of the thing you prefer. Then a sentence you might use as a **main heading** for the "By train" group could be: "Going by train has a number of advantages, of course." For the "By car" group an appropriate sentence would be: "On the other hand, the advantages of going by car far outweigh those of going by train."

Your talk should include a statement of your preference. You may want to begin by telling your classmates your decision. For example: "In spite of all the comforts of our modern railroads, I would rather make a long pleasure trip by car than by train." Or you may want to wait until the end of your talk to state your preference. For example: "Can you blame me for preferring to go by car?" Or you may do both.

Now look at the advantages you have listed. Which group will you begin with? After you have decided, think of a sentence to use as a main heading for each group. Will you express your preference in the opening sentence, in the closing sentence, or in both? Then make a final plan for your talk on a card or small piece of paper. At the top write your opening sentence. Next write the main heading for the group of advantages you will discuss first. Under it copy the details you will use, in the order in which you decided to tell them. Do the same for the second group. Then add the closing sentence.

Practice your talk at least once, timing yourself to make sure it does not take over three minutes. If called on to give your talk in class, stand well away from the desks and speak distinctly.

Expressing a Preference PART TWO: WRITTEN

You have prepared notes for an oral report in which you expressed a preference for one of two similar things. These notes will now help you in planning a written report on the same subject. How many groups of related details are shown in your notes? If you compared the advantages of two similar things, you probably have two groups of related details. Each group will be explained in a separate paragraph. Now look at the main heading you wrote for each group. Does it explain clearly how the details in the group are related? If so, you can use it for the **topic sentence** of the paragraph.

Topic sentences are particularly important when details are arranged in a logical order. Details in a time order are usually easy to  follow. When they do not come one right after the other, an expression like *That evening, The next morning,* or *Several months later* is enough to warn the reader that the next group of details will be different. And details in a space order are usually grouped according to the writer's point of view. An expression like *Ahead of me, To my left, Looking upward,* or *In the distance* shows the reader that the next paragraph is to be about a different part of the subject. But details in a logical order are grouped according to an idea in the writer's mind. Topic sentences make that idea known to the reader by explaining clearly how the details in each group are related. For example, notice the topic sentences in this plan:

	OPENING SENTENCE: In spite of all the comforts of our modern railroads, I would rather make a long pleasure trip by car than by train.
FIRST PARAGRAPH	TOPIC SENTENCE: Going by train has a number of advantages, of course.
	A. Usually faster
	B. No worry about traffic problems
	C. No worry about missing way, flat tires, gas, etc.
	D. Meals no problem—diner or club car
	E. Can stand up, stretch, wander about
	F. Can sleep in comfort—adjustable seats or Pullman

	TOPIC SENTENCE: *On the other hand,* the advantages of going by car far outweigh those of going by train.
	A. Costs less if several share expenses
	B. Can carry baggage more conveniently
	C. Can make side trips, see more scenery
SECOND PARAGRAPH	D. Can eat in different places or buy food to take along
	E. Can stop overnight at motels—with car handy
	F. No worry about reservations, schedules, transfers
	G. No porters to tip
	H. Can drive right up to destination
	CLOSING SENTENCE: Can you blame me for preferring to go by car?

The topic sentence for the first paragraph explains that the details following it will be advantages of going by train. The topic sentence for the second paragraph explains that the details following it will be advantages of going by car. Notice particularly the italicized phrase *On the other hand.* It shows the reader how the second paragraph is related to the first. A topic sentence often has two purposes: It explains how the details in the paragraph are related. It shows how the paragraph is related to the one preceding it.

Now make the plan for your composition. By means of lines or brackets indicate where each paragraph is to begin and end. Then look again at the main headings in your notes to be sure they can be used as topic sentences. If necessary, add words like *But, However, Nevertheless, In spite of these* to your second topic sentence to show its relation to the first paragraph.

When your plan is ready, write your first draft. Remember to begin the first paragraph with your special opening sentence. Follow it with the topic sentence and the first group of advantages. Then begin the second paragraph with the topic sentence and end with the last detail or with a special closing sentence. Tell each advantage clearly, keeping your classmates in mind. Try to hear your sentences as you write them down.

Revise your first draft carefully. Cross out unnecessary words; substitute exact modifiers for lazy adjectives or adverbs; vary the beginnings of your sentences; get rid of weak explanatory sentences by using appositives or verbal phrases. In short, make use of every means you have learned for improving your sentences. Then look for errors in spelling and punctuation so that you can correct them before preparing your final draft.

The title for a composition in which you express a preference for one of two similar things may be simply the names of the two things. For example:

Travel by Train and Car   Indoor and Outdoor Jobs
Biology or Chemistry?   Radio or Television

But if you want to arouse the curiosity and interest of your readers, you might use a title that merely suggests what your composition is about:

I'll Take the Highway   I'm the Outdoor Type Myself
Bugs or Bottles?   TV or Not TV, That Is the Question

When you have decided on a title for your composition, copy your revised first draft. Write as neatly as you can, and space your words so that they can be read easily. Keep margins even. Then proofread your paper for errors you may have made in copying—for words omitted or repeated, for careless misspellings and omitted punctuation marks.

Persuading Others

Unit 9

Persuading Others PART ONE: ORAL

There are various ways of persuading others to do something you want. You can coax or flatter or threaten them. You can appeal to their pride, their prejudices, their desire to go along with everybody else. Or you can appeal to their common sense—calling attention to a need that exists, winning them over to your way of thinking by giving good reasons, pointing out the advantages or benefits of doing what you recommend, and urging some definite action. Of these ways, the last is the one most likely to convince people who think for themselves.

Suitable subjects for a persuasive talk are those of personal interest to you and your classmates. In every school there are matters of general concern—suggested improvements in student government or the sports program, recommended changes in examinations or courses or assemblies or class parties. In every community there are conditions that might be remedied, activities that deserve greater support, individuals who ought to be elected to public office. If you choose a subject that is being widely discussed at the time, you will find your classmates interested in what you have to say about it. And if you choose one about which you have definite opinions, you will find it easy to plan and give a good talk. What will your subject be?

The first part of a talk in which you try to persuade others should not only suggest some action, but should make clear just why there is a need for that action. If, for example, you want others to adopt a plan for reorganizing the Student Council, you might start with a brief account of obvious faults in its present organization. If you are argu-

Unit 9 Persuading Others 55

ing for more student-produced assemblies, you might call attention to several poor programs using outside talent. Or if you want to convince others that your school should have a compulsory driver-education course, you might begin by mentioning the startling number of automobile accidents that occur every year. By beginning with what your classmates know or are willing to accept as true, you establish a common ground with them and put them in a better mood to listen to your plea for action. One of the important things you can learn about persuading others is just this: Always begin on common ground.

Once you have explained the background for the suggested action, you must convince your listeners that what you suggest is the best course to follow. You might do this in several ways—by giving reasons, by pointing out advantages or benefits, by contrasting the bad effects of not following the suggested action with the good effects of following it. In selecting details for this second part of your talk, think of your listeners. Try to foresee—and answer—their objections.

The last part of your talk should state definitely just what you hope your audience will do. For example, in a talk in which you try to convince your listeners that your plan for the reorganization of the Student Council is sound, you might ask them to vote for your plan and urge their friends to do the same. And in a talk in which you try to convince others to support the town orchestra, you might ask them to buy concert tickets, to sell tickets, and to attend the concerts.

Now make a list of all the details you will use in your talk, grouping them in three or four sections—one to give the background, one or two to explain your reasons, and one to state the action you suggest.

From your list, make the plan that you will follow in giving your talk. Arrange the details in the first section in the order that best explains the background. If there are many details in the second section, be sure to organize them in a logical order, putting related details into separate groups. If you have several details in the last section, arrange them in an effective order, perhaps placing the most important last. Your plan will have at least three groups of details—more if the second part of your talk covers more than one group of related items, as in the following plan for a talk to persuade others of the need for a compulsory driver-education course:

What is the problem?
  A. Many thousands of deaths and injuries
     caused by autos annually
  B. Bad record of teen-age drivers as compared
     with drivers of other age groups
  C. Result of publicity about teen-age reckless-
     ness—parents hesitate to teach teen-agers to
     drive or to let them use car
  D. One way of helping solve problem—insti-
     tute driver-education courses in schools

What reasons are there for teaching all high-
school students to drive?
  A. Everyone should learn how to drive—for
business, pleasure, emergencies
  B. Students without family cars should be given chance to learn
  C. Teens best time to learn; muscular coördination best
  D. Teen-agers eligible for drivers' licenses can prepare for tests
  E. Students trained in course become better pedestrians

What are the advantages of having a driver-education course as part
of the curriculum?
  A. Trained instructors more competent than relatives or friends
  B. Special training cars better than family cars for learning
  C. Movies, slides, and special equipment to show need for proper
     control of car
  D. Hand signals, traffic laws, importance of road signs taught
  E. Students also taught right attitudes—courtesy of the road, dis-
     trust of show-off and road hog, etc.
  F. Less possibility of accidents on streets and highways after
     supervised practice in blocked-off areas
  G. Tests show driver-education courses in schools cut student ac-
     cidents by 50 per cent

What can we do to get such a course for our school?
  A. Urge parents to talk about the idea and to get their clubs to
     back it
  B. Sign petition asking school board to institute course

Notice that each section of this plan has a main heading that
shows how the details are related. The main headings you use in your
plan need not be questions. They may be statements or simply phrases.
While practicing your talk, you may decide to reword the main

headings. For example, if you were making a plea for a driver-education course in your school, you might begin by saying "Let's look at the record" or "Let's face some startling facts." Instead of saying "What reasons are there for teaching all high-school students to drive?" you might begin your second group of details by saying "There are a number of reasons for giving driver-education courses to all high-school students." Or you may decide to omit one or more of the main headings, feeling that your details are so well organized that your listeners can follow your plan without them. Often it is more effective to begin directly with the first detail, especially if it was chosen to catch the attention of the audience.

If you are asked to give your talk in class, hold your notes in your hand so that you can refer to them if necessary. But remember that the less you have to depend on notes, the more convincing your talk will be.

Persuading Others PART TWO: WRITTEN

Now that you have prepared an oral composition for the purpose of persuading others, you are to prepare a written composition, using the notes you made for your talk. You know that you will have as many paragraphs as there are groups of related details in your plan. And you know that the main headings of these groups will become the topic sentences that tell the reader what the paragraphs are about.

Look at the main headings in your notes. Are they statements or questions that can be used for topic sentences? If not, how will you reword them? Remember that a good topic sentence makes it easy for the reader to know how the details in a paragraph are related.

Now write the first draft of your composition, just as you planned to tell it to your classmates. If you do not intend to use a special opening sentence, begin with your first topic sentence. Then write one or more sentences about each of the details in the first group. When you

have finished the first paragraph, refer to your notes to be sure that you have included all the details and that they are in the order you planned. Then write the topic sentence for the second group, and explain the details in that group, remembering to check with your notes after you have finished writing the paragraph. Do the same for each of the remaining groups. If you have a special closing sentence, be sure to make it part of your last paragraph. Write rapidly, trying to hear your sentences as you set them down. Use pencil and scratch paper to that you can make changes and corrections easily.

Allow ample time for revision. First, read your composition for sense, putting yourself in the place of the reader. Does the thought jump abruptly as you go from one sentence to another? Maybe you need to add words like *however* or *furthermore* to show how the sentences are related in meaning. Or maybe you have skimped one of the details in your notes and need to explain it further. Do certain sentences distract attention from the main idea of the paragraph? Perhaps you can combine them with other sentences by using appositives or verbal phrases or subordinate clauses. Occasionally you may find that such sentences are unnecessary and can be crossed out.

Next, read your first draft to yourself, listening to the sentences. Are they monotonously alike? If so, try varying them by combining some, by beginning others with something besides the subject, and by using fewer compound sentences. Always read your revised sentences over, to be sure that they are clear and make good sense.

When you have finished revising your first draft, you are ready to decide on a title for your composition. You may, of course, choose a title that simply tells what your composition is about:

> Should Our Student Council Be Reorganized?
> The Community Orchestra Needs Your Support
> Driver Education for Every Student

Or you may wish to choose a title that will catch the attention of your readers by arousing their curiosity:

> Let's Counsel Our Council
> Who Should Pay the Village Piper?
> Horse Sense Makes Horsepower Safer

As soon as you have selected a title, make a final copy of your composition to hand in. Copy accurately. Keep margins even, and write as legibly as you can. Proofread your work carefully.

If you are asked to read your composition aloud in class, read slowly and clearly enough for all to hear.

More Theme Topics

Telling about Books

No doubt you have had experience in giving book reports in which you identified the book title, told a few interesting facts about the author, explained briefly the setting, gave a summary of the plot, and perhaps ended with a sentence telling what you thought of the book. Such reports are useful and informative. But they are not the only way of telling about books. More enjoyable, sometimes, are informal talks in which you express your opinions about some of the characters or incidents in a book you have read recently.

Whether or not your classmates have read the book you choose to tell about in your informal talk is not important. Their interest will be primarily in your ideas, in your reaction to the book. Whatever the book—a novel, a biography, a collection of short stories or essays—the only requirements are that you have thought about it and are willing to share your thoughts with others.

You might, for example, tell about a character that impressed you. What are your feelings about this character? What did the character do to cause these feelings? Or you might select several incidents that seem to you worth remembering. What are they about? Why do you think they are interesting? As you can see, a book talk is concerned less with facts about a book than with your enjoyment and appreciation of it.

What will you tell about in your book talk? When you have decided, make a plan for your talk. In your plan you should make clear not only your opinion, but your reasons. For example, suppose you were telling about your reaction to Jerry Cruncher, one of the characters in Charles Dickens's novel, *A Tale of Two Cities*, which you and your classmates had read. You might feel that Jerry is not all bad, as you first thought, but that he has some good in him. By showing how your impression of him changed, you can share this feeling with others. By reminding them of specific incidents in the book, you can make clear what caused this feeling. Your plan, then, might look like this:

My first impression was that Jerry Cruncher was wholly bad.
   A. Nagged constantly at Mrs. Cruncher
   B. Unjustly accused her of being bad wife and mother
   C. Threw boot at her to stop her praying
   D. Ordered Jerry, Jr., to spy on his mother
   E. Beat her head against headboard of bed
   F. Spent money needed for household at taverns
   G. Engaged in a secret, criminal job—grave robbing
   H. Overjoyed on learning that young Jerry admires him for grave robbing
Later developments made me feel Jerry was—in his own way—as heroic as Sydney Carton.

   A. Came to the aid of friends, though by so doing had to disclose secret, thereby losing job
   B. Begged employer not for another chance for himself but for job for young Jerry
   C. Helped friends, at risk to himself, to escape from revolutionaries
   D. Promised to give up grave robbing and find honest way to earn living
   E. Promised to stop mistreating his wife

Or perhaps you have read something no one else in the class knows. For example, if you were telling about the incidents that most impressed you in a selection from a biography that only you had read, your plan might look like the one on the next page:

What I read and my opinion of it
  A. "Sailor Jack Turns Author"—selection from *Sailor on Horseback*
  B. Irving Stone's biography of Jack London, famous author of Gold Rush days
  C. Opinion—story of London's life just as fascinating and colorful as any of his tales of the Yukon
Most exciting incident—shooting White Horse Rapids
  A. Making the flat-bottom boats designed by London
  B. Deciding to attempt crossing the rapids
  C. Shooting the rapids
  D. Taking other boats through
Funniest incident—discovering "gold"
  A. Finding shining dust in gravel dug from creekbed
  B. Staking claims and spreading the news
  C. Building air castles
  D. Learning that shining dust was mica—not gold

Notice that the first group of details in this plan provides background material as well as a statement of your opinion. Usually some background is needed when your talk is about a book that your audience is not familiar with. Two or three sentences are usually enough to explain what the book is about and what you think of it.

When you have written out the plan for your talk, add good beginning and ending sentences. Then practice your talk at least once to make sure that you can give it in three minutes or less. Try to move smoothly from one detail to another, and from one group of details to another.

If you are called on to give your talk in class, stand easily but firmly on both feet, well away from any desk or chair you might be tempted to lean against. Give an impression of being at ease by occasionally turning your head from side to side so that you can look at all members of the class. Let your voice show your interest and enthusiasm. Both are contagious.

Since your teacher may ask you to turn in a copy of your notes, be sure that it is written out neatly and legibly.

Telling a Secret Ambition

Few topics of conversation are more interesting than those centering around secret ambitions we have had—and sometimes still have. Almost every small boy has at some time or other wanted to be a policeman or a fireman or a locomotive engineer. And many little girls have wanted to be nurses or teachers or ballet dancers. As we grow up, new interests may cause us to discard our earlier ambitions or may make us more determined than ever to carry them out. Whether we are afraid others will laugh at us for having these secret ambitions or whether we fail to realize how common they are, we seldom discuss them with others or even examine our own feelings about them. Yet almost everybody is interested in the secret ambitions of others, par-

ticularly when he finds out that they are not very much different from his own.

What are your secret ambitions? Have you discarded any of them as you have grown up? Have you acquired new ones that have taken the place of earlier ones? If you are a girl, you may have recently decided on a career as a social worker or a model or a skating star. If you are a boy, you may be dreaming of flying a commercial airliner or playing major-league baseball or discovering new scientific facts in a great laboratory. Whatever the ambition, you may be sure that others who know you will be interested in hearing you tell about it. Of course, it should be an ambition that you have really had or still do have. If you merely invent some outlandish ambition just to make the class laugh, your insincerity may cause others to wonder what your real ambitions are.

When you have selected a secret ambition to talk about, you are ready to plan what you are going to say. What caused you to have the ambition? How long have you had it? What do you think of it now? If you have discarded it, what were

64

your reasons? If you still have it, how do you plan to carry it out? These questions are merely to start you thinking of some of the things you might say about your secret ambition. You will, no doubt, think of many other things as you plan your talk.

Prepare your notes carefully, arranging the important details in a time order or a logical order. Be sure to list examples and reasons that you want to include in your talk. Then add good beginning and ending sentences.

Practice your talk at least once before coming to class, so that you will know what you are going to say and exactly how you want to say it. If you are asked to give your talk in class, speak slowly and distinctly. Hold your notes so that you can glance at them easily. If your classmates are amused by something you say, always wait for them to finish laughing before you continue. Your notes will remind you of what comes next. Stand squarely on both feet, and look at your classmates as you are speaking.

When others are giving their talks, pay close attention so that you can tell what you liked about their talks and what you think might be improved. Be alert for touches of humor, but be sure they are intentional. You do not want to hurt a classmate's feelings by laughing at something he is sincerely interested in. If you always show the same courtesy when others are speaking that you expect when it is your turn to talk, you will find that telling about secret ambitions is as interesting as a conversation among friends.

Telling about Interesting Jobs

If you needed a new dress or a new suit for some special occasion, would you wait until the last minute and then dash into the store nearest your home and buy the first one the clerk showed you? Or would you start "shopping around" long before the special day so that you would have plenty of time to inspect the wares in a number of stores, compare prices and values, and decide which of several things was best for you? If you are like most people, you do not make important decisions without considering all the possibilities, comparing advantages and disadvantages, getting competent advice. One of the most important decisions you will some day have to make is the choice of a vocation. It is too early, of course, for you to make a final decision. But it is not too early for you to start "shopping around" to see what jobs there are.

For this composition assignment you are to tell your classmates about a job that you think is interesting. It may be the job of a

friend or relative—a mechanic, a receptionist, a model, a football coach, a baseball umpire, a dancing teacher, a dentist, a clerk, an airline hostess, a newspaper reporter. Or it may be a job you have been reading about—that of an FBI agent, a forest ranger, a research worker, an astronomer, a dress designer, a sandhog, a lion tamer. Your talk should cover three main points: what the job is, what advantages and disadvantages it has, and what you think about it as a possible vocation.

In describing the job, you will want to give as complete a picture as you can. Just what does the worker do? How many hours does he work? Is the work well paid? What are the qualifications necessary for getting and holding the job? Try to avoid broad, vague statements; your classmates want to know specific details. In telling about the job of a clerk in a department store, for example, you might explain that clerks have other duties besides waiting on customers. They keep shelves and counters neat and clean, arrange merchandise displays, put price marks on all articles, keep close check on the stock, unload merchandise, keep daily records of their sales, attend staff meetings, and keep records of the hours worked.

To help you get started in planning the second part of your talk, you might consider questions like these: Are working conditions pleasant or unpleasant? Is the work dangerous? Is it monotonous or varied? Is it steady or seasonal? Does the worker get such company benefits as health and accident insurance, retirement pay, discounts on merchandise, paid vacations, profit-sharing payments? Does the job have other rewards besides money? For example, does it give the worker a chance to meet interesting people, to travel, to get more education? Is there any chance of advancement? Is the job easy to get, or is the field crowded? Are the rewards worth the preparation necessary to qualify for the job?

Once you have described the job and have pointed out its advantages and disadvantages, you are ready to tell your classmates in two or three sentences your opinion of the job as a vocation. Do you think it is a job you would like to have for the rest of your life? For part of your life? Not at all? Why? Is it because of its advantages? Because of its disadvantages? Or is it in spite of its disadvantages? In spite of its advantages?

Since your talk will include many details, it is important that you prepare your plan carefully, arranging the details in a logical order. Try to think of a good beginning sentence, one that will make your classmates want to hear the rest of your talk. A special closing sentence is not needed; simply end with the statement of your opinion.

Telling about Our Community

The community in which we live is all too often taken for granted. Because we have grown up in it, we seldom think to explore it for interesting facts. We open a faucet and let the water run without wondering where it comes from, how it gets into our homes, why we are able to drink it safely, or where it goes after passing down the drain. We attend the community's schools, ride on its streets, walk on its sidewalks safely at night, admire its fire engines dashing by, picnic and play ball in its parks without so much as a single thought about what makes these conveniences possible. We attend church, go to the movies, borrow books from the library, mail letters at the box on the corner, shop in the stores, ride back and forth on buses or streetcars, watch people going to work in offices or factories, and never stop to consider how these things came to be in the community.

Communities vary greatly in size, of course, from large cities to small towns and still smaller villages. Yet in almost every community there are interesting facts to discover and unusual things to talk about, if you are only willing to go exploring and to ask questions.

Have you ever thought about other schools in the community and wondered how many boys and girls attend them? Do you know how many churches there are and how many faiths are represented by them? Are there any historical points of interest? What can you tell about the fire department, the police department, the health department? Who installed the street lights and keeps them in operation? How many parks or playgrounds are there? Where is the post office, and what services does it offer? How many banks or stores or factories are there? What things are made or grown or produced in the community? Can you tell what charity organizations or service clubs or Boy Scout troops there are? If there is a transportation system, do you know how many miles its routes cover or how many buses or streetcars it operates? Can you give the number of telephones in the community or explain how the electricity in your home is made and brought there for your use?

These questions are merely to start you thinking about the community in which you live. Look at it thoughtfully. Try to find something about it that really interests you, something that arouses your curiosity, and—if possible—something that no one else in your class wants to investigate. Do not try to tell about many things. Choose one that you think will interest your classmates and plan to tell all the details you can about it.

Once you have decided what to talk about, your next step is to get the information. Write down all the questions you can think of and the names of people who might know the answers. Then talk to your teachers and your parents, asking them what they know about the subject and where to go for more information. Follow up their suggestions. Keep at it until you have as many interesting facts as you can get in the time available.

After you have collected your information, look over your facts carefully. Which ones are new to you? Which ones do you think will interest your classmates? Unless you have very little information, it is often wise to ignore facts that everybody knows and to concentrate on the things that seem most unusual.

Prepare your notes carefully, arranging the important facts in a time or space or logical order. Include exact dates, figures, or names that you think are worth mentioning. Then add good beginning and ending sentences.

Practice your talk at least once before coming to class, so that you will know what you are going to say and how you want to say it. If you are asked to give your talk in class, speak slowly and distinctly. Hold your notes so that you can glance at them easily, but try not to wave them around or look at them more than necessary. Watch your audience as you talk, shifting your eyes from one classmate to another.

Suggested Topics for Speaking and Writing, Units 2-9

Unit 2   Telling What Happened

An amusing incident
A narrow escape
An embarrassing moment
An unforgettable happening
An enjoyable experience
A strange encounter
An exciting occurrence
An unusual event
A serious mistake
A day to be remembered

My first job
My first fight
My first date
My first dance
My first circus
My first football game
My first bad scare
My first public appearance
My first formal party
My first trip away from home

Unit 3   Telling How Something Looks

A strange city
A busy harbor
A famous landmark
A shopping district
An unusual building
A national monument
Approaching the airport
America the beautiful
The home of a friend
My room

A memorable sunset
An impressive sight
A view by moonlight
A gloomy spot
A winter night
A spectacular storm
An unforgettable scene
An ideal camping place
My favorite theater
High water

70

Unit 4 *Telling About Interesting People*

Often interesting people come across in the context of an amusing anecdote. Here are a few general suggestions:

A bright remark
A clever quip
A sarcastic reply
An amusing answer
A sharp retort

A quick comeback
A cynical observation
A wise comment
A witty rejoinder
A serious thought

Unit 5 *Telling How to Make or Do Something*

How to enjoy a hobby
How to play a game
How to find a job
How to take care of a pet
How to prevent fires
How to knit a sweater
How to make candy
How to sail a boat
How to grow flowers
How to judge poultry

How to build a model airplane
How to make a dress
How to paint a picture
How to budget an allowance
How to treat a minor injury
How to learn to swim
How to trim a Christmas tree
How to organize a club
How to make a bracelet
How to develop photographs

Unit 6 *Telling What Something Means*

Success
Faith
Egotism
Courage
Honesty
Selfishness
Humor
Optimism
Reverence
Tolerance

School spirit
Good sportsmanship
Good manners
Individual liberty
Collective bargaining
Free enterprise
Intelligent patriotism
Freedom of speech
Freedom of worship
The American way of life

Unit 7 Expressing an Opinion

Why I like music
Why I like science
Why I like camping
Why I like housework
Why I like swimming
Why I dislike gossip
Why I dislike shopping
Why I dislike modern art
Why I dislike poetry
Why I dislike comic books

Why I prefer studying in a group
Why I prefer traveling by car
Why I prefer living on a farm
Why I prefer science courses
Why I prefer square dancing
Why I take part in athletics
Why I go to church
Why I belong to the Scouts
Why I makes my own clothes
Why I want to attend college

Unit 8 Expressing a Preference

Two schools
Two cities
Two hobbies
Two sports
Two occupations
Dogs and cats
Beef and dairy cattle
Trains and planes
Radio and television
French and Latin

City and country life
Electric and gas ranges
Hard and soft rock music
Soccer and football
Antique and modern furniture
Chain stores and independents
Educational and commercial televisio
Boys and girls
Drive-in and walk-in theaters
Republication and Democratic parties

Unit 9 Persuading Others

_____ should be legalized.
_____ should be abolished.
_____ is the best day.
_____ should be elected.
_____ is bad for kids.
_____ should be changed
    at my school.

You *can* trust people.
I have my rights too.
Life today is better than ever.
_____ is the best form of governm
Every student should take _____.
America should _____.

72

II. WORKING WITH PARAGRAPHS

What Makes A Good Paragraph?

Just as words are put together in many ways to make sentences—some good and some poor—so sentences may be written in paragraph groups. By understanding the various functions that sentences have in paragraphs, you can learn what makes a good paragraph and what you can do to improve a poor one. For, as you know, writing good paragraphs is more than just starting every third or fourth sentence on a new line, indenting the first word.

In the written composition lessons you have learned that a paragraph usually consists of two or more sentences that are related in some way. And you have also learned that sometimes a topic sentence helps the reader know what that relationship is. For example, here is a simple paragraph from an article on baseball:

> The hold that baseball has on the American people is well illustrated by the testimonial rite known as the Day. During a season, on the sand lots as well as in the major and minor leagues, groups of admirers honor certain players with a Lefty Smith Day or a John Jones Day. The blushing hero is showered with money, automobiles, farm machinery, jewelry, plaques, loving cups, and speeches by civic leaders. A laborer with a large family and a small income is delighted to contribute a dollar or two to such a cause. The fact that the honored player already owns two automobiles and earns a whacking salary does not deter the committee in charge of his Day.

The first sentence tells what the paragraph is about and is a topic sentence. The remaining four state facts and opinions that tell what "the Day" is and what the writer thinks of it. These are the details used to develop the paragraph. Because the five sentences are related, they work together as a group to explain one idea.

Now look at the next example, two paragraphs from an article on new developments in the making of glass:

> (1) Perhaps one of the greatest achievements of the glass scientists is "tempered glass," that has made the saying "as brittle as glass" as out of date as last week's teen-age slang. (2) Tempered glass is five times stronger than ordinary glass, being one half as strong as steel and three times more elastic, or "stretchy." (3) It can be bent and twisted without breaking, and it will not shatter when molten lead is poured onto an ice-cold slab of it. (4) Once, in a playful mood, scientists laid a piece of tempered glass between two platforms and let a full-grown elephant stand on it. (5) The glass sagged a little, but did not break.
>
> (6) Tempered glass is made by lowering a sheet of ordinary glass into a furnace. (7) When it is so hot that it is about ready to soften, the glass is removed and rapidly cooled by blowing a stream of air across it. (8) This rapid cooling gives the glass an extremely hard "skin" on either side of the plate. (9) The rest of the glass is held in tight compression between these two skins.

The sentences have been numbered for convenience in referring to them. For example, Sentence 1 is the general statement that tells what the first paragraph is about. Sentences 2 and 3 give facts that explain how tempered glass differs from ordinary glass. Sentences 4 and 5 together are one illustration of the difference. In other words, the first paragraph consists of a general statement and three details—two sentences that give facts and two that give an illustration. Notice that the order of these details is not particularly important. If Sentences 4 and 5 —the illustration—came before 2 and 3, the paragraph would still make sense. Notice, too, that even if one of the three details were omitted, you would still have a fairly good idea of what tempered glass is.

Now look at the second paragraph. Sentence 6 tells what the paragraph is about and gives the first important step. Sentence 7 gives the second important step. Sentences 8 and 9 tell the result of the treatment described in Sentences 6 and 7. Notice that the last three sentences depend on the meaning of those preceding. If the order of the details were changed or any one of the details were omitted, the paragraph would not make sense.

Both paragraphs in the example are developed by means of details, but in different ways. The details in the first paragraph are **cumulative**. Though each has to do with tempered glass, they are practically independent of one another; and the writer might have used fewer sentences or arranged them in some other order. The details in the second paragraph are **consecutive**. Because they depend on one another, the sentences must be in a certain order, and no sentence can be omitted. These are two common ways of developing paragraphs.

As you know, a paragraph is about some one idea—one part of an incident or a description or an explanation or an expression of opinion. But there are no rules about how many details are needed to make that one idea understandable. One detail may be adequate for a simple idea. Ten may not be too many for a difficult idea. How many to use is the writer's decision. If he selects enough helpful details and arranges them wisely, he will very likely succeed in making his idea clear to the reader. When that occurs, he knows that he has written a good paragraph.

Improving paragraphs
1. Have I selected details carefully?

In the written composition lessons preceding this Unit, you have learned the importance of revising first drafts to make your sentences clearer, more forceful, more interesting to read. Now you will see some of the ways in which thoughtful revision can help you improve your paragraphs.

You know that details are used to make clear the central idea of a paragraph and that they should be related in meaning. When these related details are carefully selected, they help the reader understand the idea expressed by the paragraph. When they are not, the reader may be confused. For example, what is the central idea of the following paragraph?

(1) Among pedal-propelled vehicles the bicycle is most popular. (2) True, the one-wheeled monocycle is occasionally seen in circus acts. (3) This strange-looking device is difficult to balance and steer, however, since there are no handle bars and you can fall in any direction. (4) Also, residential sidewalks are often made dangerous by small children on tricycles. (5) These small three-wheelers are easy to ride, since there is no problem in balancing them and little practice is needed to steer and pedal them at the same time. (6) But far more common is the bicycle, seen almost everywhere and ridden by young and old alike. (7) There are special racing models and lightweight touring models and the sturdy, brightly painted, chrome-trimmed "bike" that is the perennial favorite of the junior-high set. (8) The trick of balancing these popular two-wheelers is to turn the front wheel in the direction in which you start to fall. (9) Almost anyone can learn it.

Is the writer trying to tell about the popularity of the bicycle or to compare the difficulty of riding the various vehicles? You cannot be sure because the details in Sentences 2, 4, 6, 7 are about one idea, while those in Sentences 3, 5, 8, 9 are about another. As you can see, the details are all related in meaning, but they were not carefully selected to help the reader understand the idea expressed in the first sentence.

The writer had a plan that listed the following details for the paragraph: monocycles for circus performers; tricycles for children; bicycles for everyone; models for special purposes; most popular model. But in writing the paragraph, he somehow started thinking about riding the various vehicles and added details about this new idea. Thoughtful revision would have helped him eliminate these distracting details. It might also have enabled him to select additional details that showed his plan more clearly:

(1) Among pedal-propelled vehicles the bicycle is most popular. (2) True, the one-wheeled monocycle is occasionally seen in circus acts, and residential sidewalks are often made dangerous by small children on tricycles. (3) But far more

common is the bicycle, seen almost everywhere and ridden by young and old alike. (4) For racing, there are special models with narrow tires and high sprocket ratios to give utmost speed. (5) For touring, there are lightweight models with ingenious gear shifts and hand-operated brakes. (6) Most popular, however, is that perennial favorite of the junior-high set—the sturdy, brightly painted, chrome-trimmed "bike" with balloon tires, coaster brake, electric light and horn. (7) So great is the popularity of these two-wheelers in some neighborhoods that long racks for parking them may be seen near schools, libraries, and movie theaters.

If you compare the revised paragraph with the first draft, you will see that many new details have been added. But notice that they help the reader understand more clearly the idea expressed in the first sentence.

The details in the paragraph about the bicycle are cumulative. As you revise paragraphs of your own containing such details, ask yourself questions like these: Have I selected the best details I know to help the reader understand the central idea of the paragraph? Are there any distracting details that should be omitted? Should I add more details to make clear what I mean? Have I arranged my sentences in the best possible order?

Paragraphs made up of consecutive details are somewhat easier to check because the details depend more closely on one another. But questions like the following may reveal weak spots that need improvement: Have I given all the important steps? Are they in the proper order? Have I selected details that will make each step clear to the reader? Have I made clear the relationship of each sentence to the one preceding?

Such questions help you criticize your own writing thoughtfully —the first step in learning to revise your paragraphs. But remember that the purpose of this revision is not to make changes, but to improve your writing so that others can more easily understand your exact meaning.

EXERCISE 1. The following selection from a letter contains ideas just as they came to the writer's mind. Read the letter. Then rewrite it, organizing the ideas into three or four paragraphs. Select details carefully, omitting any that do not belong in the paragraphs you choose. Revise sentences wherever you need to. Be sure that each paragraph is about one idea. For example, the first paragraph might be about Uncle Ed's farm. What will the others be about?

I would have written sooner, but we've been visiting at Uncle Ed's farm. He's over fifty, but full of pep and hasn't a gray hair on his head. It's a dairy farm, and there are lots of cows. I've even learned the difference between Holstein and Jersey cows! The trip out was pretty tiring. We started as early as we could every morning and drove until dark. So there just wasn't any time to write letters. I'll never forget driving through the mountains, though. The scenery was wonderful. Uncle Ed is more fun than a circus. He's always laughing and thinking up things for us to do. One afternoon we went fishing, and Dad caught two big brook trout. That made him feel pretty good, particularly since Uncle Ed had no luck at all. But he just laughed about it and kidded Dad about "beginner's luck." We eat our breakfasts on a large screened-in porch opening off the dining room. Did you know that the cream from Jersey cows is almost as yellow as butter? We have it on our cereal every morning. It's so thick Dad says you ought to spread it on instead of trying to pour it! Uncle Ed's house is as big as a barn—not his barn, of course, but the kind we see around home. His barn is about a block long, with concrete floors and fluorescent lights and everything painted white. It looks like a hospital. You ought to see the kitchen here. It's enormous, about right for a restaurant, but Aunt Nelly says it takes a lot of cooking to keep Uncle Ed filled up. He's a big man, all right, and likes a lot of space to move around in, and his house is a huge, rambling, two-story affair with wide screened-in porches, a big stone fireplace, and rooms about the size of our classrooms at school. We'll probably be staying here for at least another week or so before starting back. I'm all for it myself, since Uncle Ed promised to take me along in his plane the next time he flies to town. He says the farmers out here use planes about the same way we use cars at home. It surely must save a lot of time, and there are plenty of places to land. I'll tell you all about it when I get back home. That ought to be the latter part of August. Let's hope the return trip will be less tiresome.

Suggested answers to the above exercise and other exercises in "Working the Paragraphs" are listed after Unit 20, beginning on page 133.

Developing the Idea

Unit 12

You have learned that a paragraph is about one idea. And you saw that sentences may either tell what the idea is or give details that help the reader understand the idea. Now you are going to see that sentences in a paragraph may have still another function, which enables the writer to develop an idea more fully.

Here is a short paragraph about research at the General Electric Company. See if you can find the sentence that tells what the paragraph is about and the sentences that give the details:

(1) Certain men at G. E. will always be connected with certain scientific developments. (2) For instance, there is Langmuir, known for his work with electronic tubes and with cloud-seeding. (3) He was the first scientist in the United States employed by an industrial company to win a Nobel prize. (4) Guy Suits, working on electric arcs, has generated flames nearly twice as hot as the sun's surface. (5) Saul Dushman is an international authority on high vacuum, electron emission, and atomic structure. (6) Alexanderson, a young Swede, came to General Electric to study railway motors. (7) He ended by inventing a high-frequency alternator which gave America its real start in high-powered radio communication.

The paragraph consists of seven sentences. The first is a topic sentence that tells what the paragraph is about. Sentences 2, 4, 5, and 6 give examples—names of men whose accomplishments help you understand what the writer means by his general statement. The two remaining sentences neither make general statements nor give details supporting a general statement. Sentence 3 adds another fact about Langmuir, the first man mentioned. Sentence 7 adds another fact about Alexanderson, the fourth man mentioned. Sentences such as 3 and 7 give additional information about a detail—the third function that sentences may have in a paragraph.

You can see that the details in the paragraph are cumulative. The writer merely gives four examples that he thinks will make his idea understandable. Since the details do not depend on one another, he might have arranged them in some other order. But notice that he could not move Sentence 2 without also moving Sentence 3, or Sentence 6 without Sentence 7. Sentences that explain a detail belong with it, even though the details themselves do not depend on one another.

Now look at the following paragraph about gray wolves. See if you can find the general statement, the sentences that give the details, and the sentences that add information about the details:

> (1) Wolves seem to plan their hunting. (2) Led generally by a she-wolf, a pack scouts for prey; and when the deer, elk, caribou, or moose is found, one or two wolves will approach the animal from downwind until it is started up. (3) Then the long chase begins. (4) One wolf will follow directly behind the quarry; others take strategic positions and often head it off so that it runs in a wide circle. (5) The run may go on for many hours until the quarry tires and slows down. (6) Then a pursuer slashes at the animal's rear while others attack its head and throat. (7) Contrary to popular belief they do not habitually hamstring their prey, but usually bring it down by tearing at its flank and hind quarters, or throat. (8) But whether it stands or runs, the wolf's slashing teeth will eventually tear it down.

Sentence 1 is the general statement. Sentences 2, 3, and 6 give the details. Sentences 4 and 5 add information about the long chase, mentioned in Sentence 3. And the last two sentences explain Sentence 6, adding information about the way wolves bring down their prey.

You can see that the details in the paragraph are consecutive. Sentence 2 tells how wolves find their prey and start it up. *Then* Sentences 3, 4, and 5 tell about the chase. *Then* 6, 7, and 8 tell how the prey is brought down. The two *Then*'s show that the writer intended the details to be in a time order. Notice that Sentence 2 gives two details. Notice also that Sentences 3, 4, and 5 are about one detail.

Most paragraphs are developed by means of details—facts, opinions, examples, illustrations, and so forth, that a writer uses to help readers understand his ideas. If the details require little or no explanation, a writer may give one or more in a single sentence. If he feels that they are difficult, he may use two or more sentences to explain each one fully. The important thing is not how many sentences a paragraph has, but how well it expresses the writer's idea.

Improving paragraphs
2. Have I explained details adequately?

You know that a paragraph is a group of related sentences that work together to express one idea. And you have seen that these sentences may have different functions. For example, here is a paragraph in which the sentences have only two functions:

> The large hall in Quito, Ecuador, was filled with light and color and noise. Girl teams from the capital were playing Guayaquil teams in the basketball tournament. Downstairs the seats were filled with old and young, rich and poor. The gallery was packed with students in school uniforms, with colored caps and arm bands. Cheerleaders whipped each group into a frenzy of cheering. But the center of the gallery attracted most attention.

The first two sentences tell what the paragraph is about. The remaining four give details. As you can see, the paragraph seems sketchy and incomplete.

Earlier in this Unit you learned that sentences in a paragraph may have a third function—to explain details more fully. See how much more interesting the preceding example is when the details are adequately explained:

> (1) The large hall in Quito, Ecuador, was filled with light and color and noise. (2) Girl teams from the capital were playing Guayaquil teams in the basketball tournament. (3) Downstairs the seats were filled with old and young, rich and poor. (4) Some had hurried from their work to be there. (5) Others had come from a late afternoon party. (6) The gallery was packed with students in school uniforms, with colored caps and arm bands. (7) They called good-naturedly to the boys who worked their way up and down the stairs selling candy, bags of peanuts, and cakes. (8) They clapped and stamped noisily when one of them lost his white cap and caught it again as it was tossed back to him. (9) Cheerleaders whipped each group into a frenzy of cheering. (10) One at a time the schools took their turns, each trying to outdo the other. (11) But the center of the gallery attracted most attention. (12) There several rows of students dressed all in blue sat together; above them were rows dressed in yellow, and below them rows dressed in red. (13) At a signal from the the cheerleader, the rows began to sway slowly, the yellow to the right, the blue to the left, and the red to the right. (14) There was an instant of silence; then the crowd recognized the waving flag of Ecuador and saluted it with deafening applause.

Sentences 4 and 5 explain more about the people mentioned in the third sentence. Sentences 7 and 8 tell what the students mentioned in Sentence 6 were doing. Sentence 10 adds information about the cheering mentioned in the ninth sentence. And Sentences 12, 13, 14 explain the statement made in Sentence 11. Notice that the explanatory sentences are closely related in meaning with the sentences they follow.

Details are not sentences. Details are facts and opinions and thoughts used to make an idea clear to the reader. How many sentences are needed to explain a detail adequately depends in part on its difficulty. It also depends on the kind of sentences used. In the preceding example, for instance, the detail expressed by Sentences 3, 4, 5 might have been given in one complex sentence: "Downstairs the seats were filled with old and young, rich and poor, some of whom had hurried from their work to be there, while others had come from a late afternoon party." And if compound sentences had not been used, the final detail might have required six or seven sentences instead of only four.

As you revise your own paragraphs, ask yourself these two questions: Have I explained the details adequately? Is there anything more I can say that will make them easier to understand? Some details will probably not need an explanatory sentence. Others may need several. How many sentences you use for each detail is not important if you remember this: Whenever two or more are used, be sure that they are closely connected in meaning, so that the reader will know that they have to do with the same detail.

EXERCISE 2. The numbered sentences tell a story about an accident at sea. As you can see, almost all the sentences begin with subject and verb. Rewrite the story, revising the sentences in the ways you have learned. And group related sentences into paragraphs that will help the reader know where there is a shift in time or place or action. You will probably need four or five or six paragraphs. The first one might begin in this way: *Rainsford lay in his chair on the deck of the yacht, puffing at his favorite pipe and thinking over the events of the past week.*

(1) Rainsford lay in his chair on the deck of the yacht. (2) He was puffing at his favorite pipe. (3) He was thinking over the events of the past week. (4) He grew drowsy soon. (5) A sharp sound startled him. (6) It was off to the right. (7) His ears were trained to that sort of sound. (8) They could not be mistaken. (9) He heard the sound again. (10) Someone had fired a gun twice somewhere off in the darkness of the night. (11) Rainsford sprang up. (12) He moved quickly to the rail. (13) He was mystified. (14) He strained his eyes. (15) He could not see at all through the dense blackness, however. (16) He jumped up on the rail. (17) He thought he might see better from there. (18) His pipe struck a rope. (19) It was knocked out of his mouth. (20) He lunged for it. (21) He stretched too far. (22) He lost his balance. (23) The warm waters of the Caribbean Sea closed over his head. (24) He struggled to the surface. (25) He shouted wildly. (26) The wash of the yacht slapped against his face. (27) It made him gag and strangle. (28) He struck out in desperation after the lights of

the yacht. (29) They were rapidly receding. (30) He swam frantically for about fifty feet. (31) He stopped then. (32) He had to calm his excited nerves. (33) He knew this. (34) This was not the first time he had been in a tight place. (35) He regained his self-possession quickly. (36) He had to decide then what to do next. (37) He realized one thing. (38) There was a slight chance that someone on the yacht was still on deck. (39) This person might hear his cries. (40) He shouted with all his power for several minutes. (41) No one heard him. (42) The lights of the yacht grew fainter. (43) They were blotted out by the night soon.

Telling How Ideas Are Related

You have seen the importance of selecting helpful details and of explaining them adequately. Now you will see some of the ways in which general statements tell the reader how details in a paragraph are related. One of these ways you know well. For example, in the following paragraph you should have no difficulty in finding the sentences that give the details and the sentence that tells how the details are related:

> (1) There is a wide disagreement among authorities as to why fish strike at artificial lures. (2) Some fishermen have the idea that fish believe the lures are good to eat. (3) More realistic fishermen are of the opinion that the fish know these offerings are merely wood or rubber or fur and feathers with hooks, and are just curious about how they taste. (4) Others hold that fish are surly and cantankerous, and resent having these monstrosities paraded before them. (5) Still other anglers feel that fish strike out of anger because their intelligence has been insulted by fishermen who think that fish believe artificial bait is food.

Sentences 2-5 give four different opinions. By telling what these opinions are about, the first sentence keeps the reader from becoming confused. Beginning with a topic sentence is a common and useful way of telling how details are related.

A topic sentence is one kind of general statement. There are other kinds that may consist of two or more sentences, as in this paragraph:

> (1) Scientists do many strange things in their search for knowledge. (2) But probably none is more odd than the recent experiments of two doctors reported in "The Yale Jour-

nal of Biology and Medicine." (3) The doctors froze the tails of mice. (4) They were not trying to be unkind to the mice. (5) They were trying to get more knowledge to help in the treatment of human beings when parts of the body are frozen. (6) After freezing the mouse tails, the doctors tried different ways of thawing them out. (7) They found that the use of snow or cold water was harmful, rather than helpful. (8) Continued mild heat was not of much value, either. (9) The best results were gotten by thawing the mouse tails rapidly. (10) The very best results combined rapid thawing with the use of certain drugs.

Sentences 3 and 6 give two consecutive details. Sentences 4 and 5 explain Sentence 3, and the last four sentences add information about Sentence 6. Neither of the first two sentences is clearly a topic sentence. But together they express the writer's opinion of the experiments described in the paragraph, and are a general statement.

A general statement is usually at, or near, the beginning of a paragraph, but not always. As you know, a special opening sentence often precedes the topic sentence of the first paragraph of a composition. In a similar way, one or more details may precede a general statement, as in the following paragraph:

(1) Every once in a while you'll pick up the paper and read of a shooting accident resulting from target practice. (2) Sometimes these mishaps are caused by careless gun handling, but more often they are due to an unfortunate choice of a shooting location. (3) Of all accidents, these are the least excusable and the easiest to prevent. (4) All that is required is to transfer one's target shooting activities to a suitable range, which, besides being safer, affords much more valuable practice than does random backlot firing.

Sentences 1 and 2 give details about one kind of shooting accident and what causes it. Sentence 3 is a general statement expressing the writer's opinion. The final sentence gives a reason for that opinion.

Now look at this next example. Can you find a general statement for each paragraph?

(1) A honeybee is not even as long as your thumbnail. (2) Its brain is hardly larger than the head of a pin. (3) Its weight is so slight it would take 750,000 bees, a single-file parade five miles long, to equal the weight of a 150-pound man. (4) Yet this midget is one of the world's most valuable animals.

(5) The honey of the honeybee was Europe's chief sugar supply until after the Roman Empire. (6) Beeswax is so diversely used in industry that our native production rarely meets the demand. (7) The value of bees as carriers of pollen on farms and in orchards is beyond calculation. (8) A hundred thousand species of flowering plants are said to depend upon bees for their existence, and orchard trees increase their yield 40-fold when they have an ample supply of bees at blooming time.

In the first paragraph, Sentences 1-3 give details about the honeybee's small size. Sentence 4 is a general statement expressing an opinion the writer has about honeybees. In the second paragraph, Sentences 5-7 give details to show three ways in which honeybees are valuable. You can see that there is no general statement in the second paragraph. But notice that the details given in the second paragraph help the reader understand the opinion expressed in Sentence 4—the general statement in the first paragraph.

As you have seen, a general statement may consist of one or more sentences, may tell what the details are about or what the writer thinks of them, may occur first or last or elsewhere in a paragraph. But always the function is the same—to tell the reader how the details are related. In some paragraphs the relationship of the details is so obvious that a general statement is clearly not needed. In all others the reader is more likely to understand the idea expressed by the paragraph when there is a general statement.

Improving paragraphs
3. Do I need a general statement?

Each paragraph you write is a signal to the reader that you consider the sentences in that group to be related in some way. The easier you make it for him to see that relationship, the more likely he is to understand your ideas. For example, here are four sentences that give details about modern phonograph records:

> Nowadays phonograph records are 7 or 10 or 12 inches in diameter. They may play at 78 or 45 or 33⅓ revolutions per minute. They may have regular grooves or much narrower "microgrooves." Even the hole in the center of the record is no longer of one standard size.

As you can see, the relationship of the details is obvious, and no topic sentence is needed. But by adding a general statement, the same four sentences might be used in a paragraph about the problem encountered in buying phonograph records today:

> If you haven't bought any phonograph records for several years, you are in for a surprise. The day has gone when a phonograph record was a phonograph record and all you needed to know was the title of the selection you wanted. Nowadays phonograph records are 7 or 10 or 12 inches in diameter. They may play at 78 or 45 or 33⅓ revolutions per minute. They may have regular grooves or much narrower "microgrooves." Even the hole in the center of the record is no longer of one standard size.

With a still different general statement, the same four sentences might be used as an example of our complex—and sometimes puzzling—civilization:

> We live in a strange age. Engineers devise ways of removing the three-speed gearshift from automobiles and of putting one on phonographs. There was even a time, not many years ago, when phonograph records came in just two sizes and could be played on any machine. Nowadays phonograph records are 7 or 10 or 12 inches in diameter. They may play at 78 or 45 or 33⅓ revolutions per minute. They may have regular grooves or much narrower "microgrooves." Even the hole in the center of the record is no longer of one standard size.

Notice that the general statement in this paragraph consists of three sentences. In the preceding paragraph, it consists of two sentences.

As you have seen, different general statements express different relationships of the details in a paragraph. In revising paragraphs of your own, always stop for a moment at the end of each paragraph. Ask yourself questions like these: What is this paragraph about? Do I need a general statement to make my meaning clear to the reader? Would a different general statement make my meaning easier to understand? Such questions will help you remember that it is your responsibility to show the reader how the details you have given are related. The more you accept this responsibility, the more effective your paragraphs will be.

EXERCISE 3. Each of the numbered groups of sentences might be used as supporting details in paragraphs intended for different purposes. Read each group carefully, and think of two different ways in which the sentences might be used. Then write two general statements for each group, showing the ways in which you think the relationship of the details might be expressed. For one of the general statements for the first group you might write: *1. Wisconsin, the land of lakes, is famous not only for its resorts, but also for its dairying industry and livestock production.*

1. More than half of all the cheese made in the United States is produced in Wisconsin. One tenth of the nation's butter and one fourth of its supply of condensed and evaporated milk come from the Badger state. Malted milk, invented by William Horlick in 1882, is another leading product. Wisconsin purebred dairy cattle, noted here and abroad, are sold by the thousands to farmers in other states and in foreign countries.

2. An amateur boxing match lasts for only three rounds. The boxers wear extra large, well-padded gloves, so that the damage they can inflict is minimized. A bout is stopped immediately if a boxer has an injury that seems to be at all serious or painful, and the decision is awarded to his opponent. Since the fighters are hardly ever knocked unconscious, the possibility of their becoming "punchy" from amateur competition is remote.

3. From his easy chair Mr. John Doe can view history in the making through on-the-spot news events commented on by any one of a number of excellent news analysts. He can now see the very best entertainers from stage, concert hall, movies, opera—a whole world that has in the past been restricted to small audiences. Fine young talent, which before had no place to shine in the overcrowded field of show business, is making its debut on America's TV sets.

Clinching the Point

The following paragraph is about the director of a motion picture. As you read it, notice how each sentence adds to your understanding of his responsibility:

(1) Since the action for a movie is shot in short stretches, and not in the sequence it will follow in the finished production, it is obvious that someone must have the over-all picture in mind, must be responsible for the completed production, as a conductor is responsible for the total effect all the instruments in an orchestra will make. (2) This person is the director, and it is probable that he is the one person most responsible for whether a movie will be successful or a failure. (3) The actors do only what he tells them to do, and when. (4) It is he who decides how the story is to be told, who knows what emotional effect is necessary, and guides the actors in producing that effect. (5) It is he who must figure out what the cameras must reveal, who decides whether close-ups of one person will convey an idea better, or whether the scene should show a whole group present while a speech is being made or a feeling registered. (6) He must keep in mind all the time what the total effect of the finished film will be, and work with that effect always in mind, whereas the actors need only concentrate on what they are doing at a given moment. (7) The director, to be sure, usually has a number of assistants who take care of minor details—such as getting the extras in place for a crowd scene and coaching them as to what they are expected to do—but the final assembling of all the parts into a pleasing, effective whole is up to him.

As you can see, the first two sentences make a general statement about the idea to be developed in the paragraph. And Sentences 3-6 give details in support of that statement. Now look at the final sentence. Notice that the last part of it repeats the idea expressed by the general statement, though in different words. The paragraph could have ended with Sentence 6. But by adding Sentence 7 to restate the central idea, the writer helps you remember the point of the paragraph.

This is the fourth function that a sentence may have in a paragraph—to sum up details by restating the idea they help make clear. Such a sentence is called a **summary sentence**. Because it comes last, it helps clinch the point of the paragraph.

Sometimes a summary sentence may be more explicit than the general statement itself. Notice that this is so in the following paragraph about icebergs:

> (1) There are few objects in all nature as beautiful—or as dangerous—as icebergs, those floating monsters of the deep. (2) Breaking off from massive Greenland glaciers, these mountains of frozen water—frequently as long as a city block and rising half that high out of the ocean—are carried along by the currents. (3) Some northern bergs (for there are also bergs in Antarctic regions) reach the Labrador current and are carried by it toward the heavily traveled North Atlantic steamship lanes. (4) These bergs cannot be held back, destroyed by any method now known, or even turned from their course. (5) And so the iceberg still remains a menace that science, with all of its resources, cannot control or regulate.

When you start reading, it is not clear from the general statement in the first sentence whether the paragraph is about the beauty of icebergs or about their danger. However, the details in Sentences 2-4 suggest the latter. And the final sentence removes all doubt by stating that the iceberg is a menace. Here the summary sentence is desirable for clearness as well as for emphasis. Because it follows the details, it can make a definite statement that might not have been fully understood earlier in the paragraph.

Occasionally a summary sentence will refer to a sentence in a preceding paragraph. This is likely to occur when the two paragraphs are closely related, as they are in this example:

(1) In speaking of a telescope, people often ask, "How much does it magnify?" (2) Actually, you can vary the magnification of a telescope by using different eyepieces; and practically all telescopes, even homemade ones, are arranged so that the eyepieces can be changed. (3) "But," you may ask, "if you can get a high magnification with a small telescope, what is the need of a large one?"

(4) There is a very good reason, you will discover, for building large telescopes. (5) For any given size, there is a practical limit to the magnification that can be used successfully. (6) As you know, the objective lens, or the concave mirror, gathers light to form the image, which is then magnified by the eyepiece. (7) The more the image is magnified, the fainter the light becomes. (8) It is like trying to spread a large piece of bread with a very small bit of butter. (9) You need more butter! (10) And to produce a high magnification in a telescope, you need more light! (11) How do you get it? (12) By using a larger objective or mirror, which will gather more light in. (13) So, you see, large telescopes are needed, after all.

As suggested by the general statement in Sentence 4, the second paragraph is an answer to the question asked in the first one. Starting with Sentence 5 and ending with Sentence 12, the writer gives a series of consecutive details explaining the "very good reason" mentioned in Sentence 4. Because the explanation is long and involved, the writer adds a summary sentence to remind you of the point of the paragraph. But notice that Sentence 13 refers more directly to Sentence 3 than to Sentence 4. In this way the writer not only sums up the details of the second paragraph, but also emphasizes its close relation to the first one.

As you have seen, summary sentences are used to call attention to the central idea of a paragraph. They may simply state this idea in a different way. They may state it in a more definite way. But they always refer to an idea that has been previously expressed. If you remember this, you will not be likely to confuse a summary sentence with a general statement placed last in the paragraph. A summary sentence always restates.

4. Do I need a summary sentence?

You know that a general statement helps the reader understand the central idea of a paragraph. And you have just seen some of the ways in which a summary sentence helps the reader remember this idea. The more closely the general statement and the summary sentence work together, the more effective the paragraph is likely to be.

A summary sentence is sometimes more specific than the general statement, as in the following paragraph:

> A blurred image on the film may be caused in various ways. Probably the commonest cause of blurred images is movement of the camera during the exposure of the film. Another common cause is inaccurate focusing of the lens. A third cause of blurring, which occurs in photographing moving objects, is use of a shutter speed that is too slow. Only when sufficient care is given to keeping the camera steady, to focusing the lens accurately, and to selecting a shutter speed that will "stop the action" can the film record an image that is sharp and clear.

The first sentence of the paragraph tells how the details are related. The final sentence not only sums up the details, but tells what must be done to secure sharp images. A summary sentence is often used in this way to make the meaning of a paragraph more definite.

Earlier you saw that the same details might be used with different general statements to express different ideas. For example, here is a paragraph that tells how photographs depend on the quality of the negative:

> The paper print we call a photograph is made from a negative. If the image on the negative is blurred, a picture printed from it will be blurred also. Probably the commonest cause of blurred images. . . . Another common cause. . . . A third cause of blurring. . . . Thus it is apparent that if we want a sharp, clearly defined photograph, we must begin with the making of the negative.

Since the details are the same as in the first example, only the first words of each one are given. If you supply the remaining words, you will see that the details help make clear the idea expressed in the first two sentences. Notice that the summary sentence calls the reader's attention to this idea, not by summing up the details supporting it, but by stating it in another way. Notice, too, how repetition of the words *we, photograph,* and *negative* ties the first and last sentences together.

Sometimes a summary sentence calls attention to the central idea by restating it in a completely different way:

> Some people will spend sixty dollars for a good camera, yet refuse to spend sixty minutes learning to operate it properly. Then they wonder why their pictures are not always clear and sharp. Probably the commonest cause of blurred images. . . . Another common cause. . . . A third cause of blurring. . . . Violinists know that it takes more than a Stradivarius to make good music, and photographers soon discover that it takes more than an expensive camera to produce good pictures.

Here the comparison between violinists and photographers strengthens the idea that skill is needed to secure the best results from a fine instrument.

Summary sentences have one main function—to emphasize important ideas. And like all devices for indicating emphasis in writing, they are most effective when used with thoughtful care. As you read over paragraphs you have written, ask yourself questions like these: Which paragraphs express ideas that I particularly want the reader to remember? Will summary sentences make these ideas stand out more clearly? How can I word each summary sentence to make it work closely with the general statement of the paragraph? Have I used any summary sentences that can be improved? Such questions will help you use summary sentences intelligently—and effectively.

EXERCISE 4. The numbered sentences tell of some of the unusual foods prized in various parts of the world. Most of the sentences begin with subject and verb. Rewrite the account, revising the sentences to make them more clear, forceful, and interesting. Be sure to group related sentences into paragraphs that show a shift from one phase of the subject to another. You will need five paragraphs.

(1) There are many strange foreign foods. (2) We consider these foods unappetizing. (3) We shudder at the thought of eating such foods. (4) They are considered rare delicacies by native connoisseurs. (5) Such exotic dishes as shark-fin soup and snails in vinegar are among these unusual foods. (6) Another is African black ants. (7) These ants are deep fried. (8) Another exotic dish is sea-slugs. (9) We are particular about one thing in America. (10) We must have our eggs fresh. (11) Fermented eggs are highly esteemed in China. (12) These eggs are buried for long periods of time. (13) They become green then. (14) They become cheeselike. (15) The older the eggs are, the more flavorful they are considered. (16) They are considered more valuable, too. (17) There are eggs one hundred years old. (18) These might be served in the homes of the very wealthy. (19) Another Chinese luxury is bird's-nest soup. (20) This soup is made from the nests of a species of swifts. (21) These swifts build their homes high on the faces of cliffs. (22) They build their homes at the mouths of caves, also. (23) The nests are made of twigs and seaweed. (24) The birds glue the twigs and seaweed together with their saliva. (25) The twigs and seaweed are strained out and discarded. (26) The saliva is used in bird's-nest soup. (27) The nests are very hard to get. (28) The cost of them is extremely great, therefore. (29) None except the rich can afford this rare delicacy for this reason. (30) We Americans like our tea with lemon. (31) We may like cream instead. (32) The Tartars of central Asia prefer butter in their tea. (33) The Tibetans prefer this, too. (34) They are also of central Asia. (35) They use a reeking, rancid butter for this purpose. (36) It is made from yak's milk. (37) The Oriental uses this butter on his cigarettes, also. (38) This causes the cigarettes to splutter in burning. (39) It makes them emit a choking and pungent smoke, also. (40) These strange habits and these strange foods are revolting to us. (41) They disgust us. (42) Many Americans eat raw clams, rattlesnake meat, and sweetbreads, however. (43) They consider them treats. (44) Such treats would delight the palate of a gourmet. (45) Taste is just a matter of geography maybe.

Tying Paragraphs Together

Y ou know that a paragraph usually consists of two or more related details. And you have learned that when the details are arranged in a logical order, words such as *first, second, next, finally* and phrases such as *on the other hand, considering all the facts, to conclude* show how the paragraphs are related. Whenever such words and phrases are used to help the reader follow the thought as it moves from one paragraph to another, they are called **linking expressions.**

There are many kinds of linking expressions, but they all have one purpose—to tie paragraphs together. For example, as you read the following selection, notice how the italicized words help you follow the writer's thought from paragraph to paragraph:

(1) New to the housing project, Mary walked uncertainly from her doorstep to the group of children. (2) At her former home she would have skipped with anticipation, and appropriate words of greeting would have formed spontaneously. (3) Here, only her father and mother remained familiar.

(4) *Minutes later*, Mary again stood at the door. (5) Her mother noted the clenched fists and defiant face.

(6) *Within the hour* the mothers of other children in the project had heard the new little girl was rough. (7) She had seized Judy's wagon and hit Judy.

(8) *Outcast*, Mary spent the ensuing days unhappily. (9) Increased demands upon her parents and their sympathetic attempts to help her understand how it takes time to make friends left her unsatisfied. (10) Normally a happy child, eager, affectionate, playful, and occasionally tearful, Mary had become desperately lonely.

(11) *Relief* for Mary and her concerned parents came un-

expectedly. (12) A neighbor asked if Mary might accompany her and her own daughter, one of the group, for a walk in the park. (13) Mary and the little girl became friends. (14) When Mary again approached the children, she saw them in the light of her experience with her new friend and soon found a place among them.

As you can see, the five paragraphs tell about an incident, the problem it caused, and how the problem was solved. The first two linking expressions indicate lapses of time. The second two indicate shifts to other phases of the subject. Notice that each of the linking expressions is part of the general statement of the paragraph.

Sometimes a whole sentence is used as a linking expression, as in the following selection, which tells about a fruitless search for snow geese:

(1) All day we searched for snow geese. (2) Plodding along paths that wandered aimlessly across the grass marsh south of Fortesque, N. J., we flushed drake shovellers from muddy ponds and found a pair of blue-winged teal swimming in the elbow of an estuary. (3) We found black ducks, marsh hawks, snipe, and various sparrows. (4) We found, also, blind potholes by falling into them. (5) And we waded on with a hip boot full of water in search of snow geese. (6) Other birds we found, but not the geese.

(7) Sunny morning gave way to afternoon. (8) Though it was March with the snow only two weeks gone, wavering warm air made exotic the shapes of common birds. (9) In the distance gulls sunning on a black mudbank were unidentifiable, the outline of a harrier coursing over faun grass was distorted by the air, now long-necked, now long-winged, thermal waves toying with reality. (10) Every flash of a wing had to be pursued though we fell into another pothole or plowed through sucking mud. (11) In the distance one could not be sure that flickering wing belonged to a gull. (12) We took no chances on missing the geese.

(13) Yet when evening came, hazy with pinks and yellows, turning us back toward the village, we had seen no geese. (14) That our books were filled with names and notes of other choice wild fowl, our heads filled with their vivid

images, did not prevent disappointment. (15) When one looks for snow geese there is no substitute. (16) We walked back along the edge of Delaware Bay seeking the solid footing of sodded banks and hard-sand beaches, wondering why we had seen no geese.

Now look at the second paragraph. From the details you can see that Sentence 12 is the general statement. Sentence 7 merely links the second paragraph to the first. This is the fifth function that sentences may have in a paragraph—to show how the paragraph is related to a preceding one. Such a sentence is called a **transitional sentence**.

Notice that the adverbial clause *when evening came* in Sentence 13 helps tie the third paragraph to the second. Here, instead of again using a separate sentence, the writer wisely makes the linking expression part of the general statement. Variety in linking expressions is as desirable as variety in sentences.

Repetition of important words is another way of tying paragraphs together, as you can see in the following description of a coral atoll:

(1) The world contains certain patterns of beauty that impress the mind forever. (2) They might be termed the sovereign sights, and most men will agree as to what they are: the Pyramids at dawn, the Grand Tetons at dusk, the Arctic wastes. (3) The list need not be long, but to be inclusive it must contain a coral atoll with its placid lagoon, the terrifyingly brilliant sands, and the outer reef shooting great spires of spindrift a hundred feet into the air. (4) Such a sight is one of the incomparable visual images of the world.

(5) This is the wonder of an atoll—that you are safe within the lagoon while outside the tempest rages. (6) The atoll becomes a symbol to all men seeking refuge, the security of home, the warmth of love. (7) Lost in a wilderness of ocean, the atoll is a haven that captivates the mind and rests the human spirit.

(8) More than a symbol, however, the atoll is a reservoir of tangible beauty. (9) Fleecy clouds hang over it, so that in the dawn it wears a shimmering crest of gold. (10) At midday it seems to dream in the baking heat, its colors uncompromisingly brilliant. (11) At sunset the clouds once more reflect

a flaming brilliance. (12) At night stars seem to hover just out of reach, and if there is a moon it does not dance upon the lagoon. (13) Its reflection lies there passively, like a silvered causeway to the opposite shore.

Repetition of the words *atoll* and *lagoon* in Sentence 5 links the second paragraph to the first. In addition, the words *safe* and *tempest rages* suggest a contrast similar to the one expressed in Sentence 3 by the words *placid* and *great spires of spindrift*. Words such as these, which suggest a previous idea without renaming it, are often called **echo words**. They, too, help tie paragraphs together.

Notice that repetition of the words *symbol* and *beauty* in Sentence 8 links the third paragraph to the preceding ones. Notice, too, that the word *passively* in Sentence 13 echoes the idea of *placid* in Sentence 3 and helps tie the three paragraphs together.

You have seen how paragraphs may be tied together by the use of linking expressions—words, phrases, clauses, even sentences, that help the reader know how a paragraph is related to a preceding one. When the relationship is obvious, no linking expression is needed. But wherever there is a lapse of time between paragraphs, a change in point of view, a sudden shift or an abrupt turn in the thought, a suitable linking expression usually helps the reader make the transition from one paragraph to another.

Improving paragraphs
5. Have I used good linking expressions?

As you drive along a well-marked main highway, your trip is made easier by the little roadside signs that show you the way. Some warn you of turns to the left or right, of junctions with other routes, of detours from the main road. Others merely give the route number, to let you know whether you are still on the right road. Together they speed your progress, mile by mile, toward your destination.

Linking expressions are also of two kinds. There are direct expressions that guide the reader as he goes from paragraph to paragraph. Because they are used to warn him of each change in time or place, each shift in thought, they are placed near the beginning of the paragraph, usually in the first sentence. There are also indirect expressions that guide the reader by repeating or echoing important ideas, thus helping to keep him on the right track. Linking expressions of this indirect sort may occur almost anywhere in a paragraph.

Here are a few examples of direct linking expressions that might be used to introduce paragraphs in a composition:

To SHOW CHANGES IN TIME. From early childhood . . . After starting to school . . . Shortly before my tenth birthday . . . Sometime later . . . When I was twelve . . . Today . . . Next year . . . Other plans for the future . . .

To SHOW STEPS IN A PROCESS. After you have checked the pattern . . . While cutting the material . . . Next . . . In fitting the garment . . . Finally . . .

To SHOW CHANGES IN SPACE. As we climbed the ladder . . . Upon reaching the top . . . Straight ahead . . . To our left . . . On our right . . . Below . . .

To SHOW SHIFTS IN THOUGHT. Upon closer examination . . . In theory . . . Practically, however, . . . Strangely enough . . . While many may disagree . . .

Notice in each example the variety of linking expressions used. As you revise first drafts of your compositions, ask yourself questions like these: Have I used linking expressions that show the relationship of each paragraph to the one preceding? Can I express these relationships more exactly by using other linking expressions? Such questions will remind you of the importance of linking expressions. If you want the reader to understand what you write, you must help him follow the turns in your thought from the first paragraph to the last.

Indirect linking expressions also help keep the reader from losing his way, but by different means. Earlier you saw two paragraphs about the need for large telescopes. Turn back to page 95, and count the number of times the word *telescope* (or *telescopes*) occurs in each paragraph. Then notice the words *magnify* and *magnification* in the first paragraph. How many times is the verb form used in the second paragraph? How many times is the noun form repeated? You can see that the writer never lets you forget what he is talking about.

Remember that you can link paragraphs together—indirectly—in various ways: by repeating important, or "key," words (*telescope, snow geese*); by using pronouns (*this, that, these, he, they*); by using different forms (*deny, denial*); by using synonyms (*throw, toss, pitch*); and by rephrasing (*vocation, life's work, daily bread and butter, means of earning a living*).

As you revise paragraphs you have written, watch for opportunities to use linking expressions that remind the reader of important ideas. By never giving him a chance to forget what you are writing about, you help him follow your thinking closely, unerringly, to the very end.

EXERCISE 5. In a magazine you read regularly, find an interesting article that has at least ten paragraphs. Read it through carefully. Then look for direct linking expressions that helped you follow the writer's thought from paragraph to paragraph. Next see if the writer has used any indirect expressions to help link the paragraphs together. On a sheet of paper, write the name of the author, the title of the article, the name of the magazine, and its date. Then write each direct linking expression that is used. After it, in parentheses, write the indirect linking expressions—words that repeat important ideas mentioned in a preceding paragraph. Be ready to discuss your list in class.

Recognizing Paragroups

Logically, a paragraph is a distinct part of a composition. And ideally, all the details having to do with that part should be in one paragraph. But practically, a paragraph is often little more than a way of showing in writing that two or more sentences are related in some way. Use of the same word for both kinds of paragraphs is sometimes confusing, particularly so when two or more written paragraphs are used to make clear one part of a composition.

You have learned that a paragraph is about one idea. Yet if you are at all observant, you must often have noticed in your reading two or more paragraphs that seemed to be about the same idea. For example, on page 89 you saw two paragraphs about the honeybee, and your attention was called to the fact that the details in the second paragraph supported an opinion expressed by the general statement in the first one. It is obvious that the eight sentences are about one idea. Yet the writer grouped them into two paragraphs. Since the two paragraph groups have to do with one part of the composition, they may be called **a paragroup** to show that together they do the work of a single logical paragraph.

Here is another example of a paragroup in which the general statement is separated from the details supporting it:

(1) The average man in the shoes of Douglas Campbell, for instance—the lad who has been shooting tigers in India and shooting pictures under the sea—would long ago have retired to a farm to spend the rest of his days protecting his nose. (2) But Campbell goes right on sticking his nose out, and getting it smashed.

(3) He broke his nose first when he fell off a set of parallel bars in the gymnasium of the University of Southern Cal-

ifornia, where he went to swim and get an education. (4) He smashed it next when he fell into a tiger pit in India and was spiked by a piece of bamboo. (5) He broke it a third time against the cowl of a racing car he was driving around the track at Ascot, California. (6) He smeared it to pulp against the inside of his diving helmet when he came up fast and struck the boat off Cedros Island. (7) He put the finishing touches to it while driving a car through a house as a stunt for the movies. (8) It isn't much of a nose nowadays, but Campbell is still pushing it into trouble.

Sentences 1 and 2 express the general statement. Sentences 3-7 give the supporting details. Sentence 8 is a summary sentence, restating the idea expressed in Sentence 2. As you can see, the eight sentences are about one idea and could be in one paragraph. But the writer preferred to split them into two paragraph groups, separating the details from the general statement. The summary sentence shows that the two groups really do the work of a single logical paragraph.

A paragroup is often used for a comparison between two persons or things, as in the following example:

(1) Wagner and Cobb are still regarded as the best all-around ballplayers America has produced. (2) They were exact opposites. (3) Wagner—a mild-mannered, ungainly, bowlegged man—had enormous hands. (4) From his position at shortstop, he could stop practically any ball hit at the left side of the Pittsburgh infield, and from any position—on his knees or falling on his face—his throw to first base was always as straight and as fast as a rifle shot. (5) He led the National League in hitting for eight years, and he was a peerless base runner. (6) Honus always had a kind word and a smile for everybody he played against.

(7) Cobb, on the other hand, was a graceful, belligerent figure who played with a cold fury. (8) It was said that he sharpened his spikes with a razor strop. (9) Get in his way, and he'd slash you to ribbons. (10) Cobb led the American League in batting for twelve years, but he was not a slugger. (11) His hands on the bat were five or six inches apart, ready to bunt or to choke as the occasion presented itself. (12) His record of 96 stolen bases in 1915 has never been equaled.

Sentences 1 and 2 are the general statement. Sentences 3-6 give the details about Wagner. Sentences 7-12 give the details about Cobb. By splitting the details into two groups, the writer sharpens the contrast. But notice that the general statement is for the paragroup, not just the first paragraph, and both paragraphs are needed to make it clear.

Sometimes a paragroup is used to call attention to details that are more important than others. For example:

(1) Perhaps to comprehend this point fully, it is necessary to understand something of the buffalo's economic importance to the Indian, since it was primarily the buffalo which opened the bitter wedge between the two races. (2) The buffalo's hide, tanned and decorated, was used to make the lodges of the Indian. (3) Blankets and covering came from the same source. (4) The beaver, the antelope, the bear, and the wolf each contributed its small share; but these were not a dependable source, while the buffalo in its countless numbers and predictable migrations could always be relied upon. (5) Picket ropes and lariats, harness for the pony travois and dogsled; spoons and rude knives, needles and many a useful implement; horns to decorate headdresses; skulls to make masks for the medicine men—these were but some of the uses to which the buffalo was put.

(6) Most important of all, the animal meant food and sustenance, without which the Indians must perish and die. (7) Buffalo meat was the red man's principal article of diet. (8) Dried, it could be kept indefinitely; mashed into a pulp and mixed with chokeberries or wild plums and packed into parflêches (containers of buffalo hide) tight-sealed with suet, it could be kept for years on end, a reliable source of food when all others failed. (9) The marrow was used for medicine, as well as for greasing and oiling rifles. (10) The gall was a tonic. (11) In fact, there was scarcely a point in the entire scheme of Indian living where the buffalo did not play some part, great or small.

Sentence 1 is a general statement for the paragroup. Sentences 2-5 give certain details. Sentences 6-10 give other details that the writer wants to give special emphasis to. But notice that Sentence 11 sums up the details in both paragraphs and restates in part the idea expressed in Sentence 1.

You have seen three of the ways in which paragroups are used—to separate details from a general statement, to sharpen a contrast, to call attention to important details. There are other ways, some of which you will see in the Units that follow. But two things you should remember about paragroups: (1) They do not represent mere whimsy on the part of the writer. (2) They do not violate what you have learned about paragraphs; for, as you have seen, paragroups have general statements, supporting details, and summary sentences, just as logical paragraphs do.

Improving paragraphs
6. Have I grouped details effectively?

In writing from a plan, you have learned to use a separate paragraph for each group of related details. If your plan has been carefully prepared, the sentences in each paragraph will tell about one phase of your subject and so be clearly related in meaning.

As you may have discovered, however, it is often easier to arrange related details in a plan than it is to explain them in a paragraph. One group of five details may be about a simple idea that can be made clear in a paragraph of two or three sentences. Another group of five details may be about an idea so complex that two or three sentences are needed for each detail, several more for a general statement, and possibly another for a summary sentence. Such a paragraph presents a problem, since it is difficult for the average reader to follow one thought through a dozen or more sentences. Paragroups offer a practical solution to this problem.

While writing, you should of course be concerned more with expressing your ideas clearly than with keeping track of the number of sentences you use. But in revising your first drafts, you have an opportunity to notice long paragraphs that might make your composition difficult to read. When you find such a paragraph, the first thing is to ask yourself questions like these: Have I kept to the central idea of the paragraph? Have I followed a straight line throughout the paragraph? Does each sentence help to make my meaning clear? If your answer to each of these questions is Yes, you know that all the sentences are necessary. Then the next thing is to see whether you might split the paragraph into smaller groups, making a paragroup of it.

Look at the paragraph carefully. Is the general statement long? Perhaps you can separate it from the details. This is particularly useful when the general statement is made up of several sentences or is preceded by other sentences. By putting the sentences expressing the general statement in one group and those giving the details in another, you help the reader see where the general statement ends and the details begin.

Does the paragraph express a contrast? Perhaps you can separate the two items. This is often useful when there are several points of difference. By making a separate group of the sentences that have to do with each item, you help the reader keep the discussion of one item separate from that of the other.

Does the paragraph have many details? Perhaps you can put some of them into a separate group. This is usually effective when important details have been put last. By making a separate group of the sentences giving such details, you help the reader realize their importance.

In using paragroups to make long paragraphs easier to read, try to remember three things: (1) Effective paragroups do not just happen. They are made by grouping sentences according to their meaning within the paragraph. (2) The sentences are not changed in order or number. They are simply separated into smaller groups. While the sentences may be grouped in various ways, nothing is added to them, and nothing is omitted. (3) Sentences that help explain a detail belong with it. And no group should have in it explanatory sentences that belong with a detail in some other group.

Paragroups are never an excuse for slipshod paragraphing. Since the paragraphs in them look like any other paragraphs, the reader naturally expects the sentences in each group to be closely related in meaning. When they are, he can move quickly and easily from one group of sentences to the next. And this is important; for regardless of the number of groups into which they are separated, the sentences must work together to make clear the central idea of the paragroup.

EXERCISE 6. You have seen that a long paragraph is often easier to read when is it made into a paragroup. Turn to page 84, and read again the long paragraph about the large hall in Quito. How would you separate the sentences into two groups? On a sheet of paper, write "Group 1" and, after it, the numbers of the sentences you would keep in the first group. On the following line, write "Group 2" and, after it, the numbers of the sentences you would put in a second group. Then turn to page 93, and do the same for the long paragraph about the responsibility of a movie director. Be ready to discuss your reasons for dividing the paragraphs as you have.

Allocating Space

In writing, space is often a measure of importance. If half of an article tells about the way in which a new automobile runs, while only a quarter of the article tells how it looks, you assume that the writer considers the performance of the car more important than its appearance. It does not matter whether the half is five hundred words out of a thousand, or fifty out of a hundred. What does matter is the proportion—that twice as much space is used to tell about one quality as about the other.

The following selection tells about the public appearances, the daily routine, and the physical appearance of a young violinist. Notice how the amount of space allocated to each idea affects your impression of its relative importance:

(1) The young violinist made his first public appearance when his teacher, Galamian, presented his pupils in a recital at Town Hall, May 19, 1947. (2) Late in 1948, when only twelve, Michael was soloist with the Rhode Island Philharmonic symphony orchestra for five concerts in Rhode Island cities.

(3) In January, 1949, Michael gave a concert at Plateau Hall, Montreal, Canada, and shortly afterwards won the Edgar Stillman Kelley scholarship of $250 yearly for three years in competition with other young musicians representing eleven northeastern states. (4) Later on Michael appeared as soloist under the baton of Leon Barzin for the Carnegie Hall children's concert that featured 146 young musicians from New York schools. (5) And soon after, he played in Cuba with the Havana Philharmonic symphony under the direction of Artur Rodzinski.

(6) Michael begins his day at 7 a.m. and spends from fifteen to thirty minutes practicing scales before breakfast. (7) Despite the many hours he practices, he finds time to play ping-pong and collect stamps. (8) He is a good swimmer and enjoys this sport and bicycle riding.

(9) Michael has jet black hair and dark brown eyes. (10) His height and weight are debatable because he outgrows his suits between concerts.

By devoting almost two thirds of the space to the public appearances, the writer shows which idea he considers of greatest importance. By using approximately one eighth of the space to tell about Michael's appearance, he shows which idea he considers of least importance.

The principle of allocating a larger proportion of space to a more important idea applies also to details, as in the following selection:

(1) Most Australians—figuratively speaking—live off the backs of sheep. (2) Australia is the greatest wool-producing (and wool-exporting) country in the world. (3) One sixth of all the sheep in the world are in Australia. (4) She has no fewer than 115,000,000 sheep—nearly 14 sheep per inhabitant!

(5) And lucky it is for Australia. (6) For today there is a record-breaking boom in wool. (7) Wool prices have shot up to an all-time high. (8) The reason is the expanding size of armies throughout the world. (9) The armed forces require large quantities of wool for uniforms and blankets.

(10) Second in importance to wool is wheat. (11) Australia is a leading wheat-growing country. (12) Other crops are oats, barley, corn, potatoes.

(13) Industrially, Australia has made remarkable progress. (14) Its manufacturing output tripled from 1915 to 1940. (15) During World War II, the country served as the "arsenal" for the Allies in the South Pacific theater.

(16) And since the end of the war, the pace has been kept up. (17) Industry has been operating in high gear. (18) Employment generally is at peak levels. (19) About 3,250,000 people are gainfully employed—which is a huge percentage of the total population.

By using ten lines to tell about wool and only three lines to tell about the other products, the writer leaves you in no doubt as to which of the agricultural products he thinks is most important. And by giving nine lines to industry, he indicates roughly his opinion of its importance as compared with agriculture. Notice that space is here a guide to the relative importance not only of two main parts, but also of the details in one of those parts.

You know that after an idea has been explained once, there is less need for explaining it fully each time it is repeated. As you read the next selection, notice the decreasing emphasis given to the idea of turning a dream into reality:

(1) In Missouri, a man stood looking over the ugly expanse of a city dump. (2) But he didn't see the rusting cans, the heaps of rubbish. (3) What he saw, instead, was a city of incomparable beauty where people would live in gardened houses along sweeping drives.

(4) It was a wild dream, yet amazingly he made it come true. (5) Today, on the site of that dump, there is a city where 50,000 people live in a parklike atmosphere.

(6) In California, another man walked through a sunbaked barley patch and looked down a dusty country road. (7) "Here," he said, "is the place for the most beautiful shopping street in the world." (8) Another dream, but it, too, came true. (9) That dirt road is now a fabulous stretch of boulevard, the "Fifth Avenue of the West."

(10) In New York City, a third man studied the monotonous piles of brick and stone that rose above the paving. (11) "Do city apartments have to be like that?" he asked himself. (12) "Why can't we have trees and lawns and children's playgrounds right here in Manhattan?" (13) Though he was old and ready to retire, he rolled up his sleeves and turned another dream into reality.

(14) These men were called crazy idealists, yet they lived to see their visions show the way to better living for everyone in America. (15) Some were real-estate men who saw beyond mere subdivisions; some were builders who found better ways to build homes; others were businessmen who dared to invest huge sums in a new kind of enterprise.

To explain that the first man made his dream come true, the writer uses two sentences (4 and 5) and sets them off as a separate paragraph. To explain that the second man realized his dream, the writer again uses two sentences (8 and 9) but this time keeps them a part of the paragraph. To explain that the third man turned a dream into reality, the writer uses only part of Sentence 13.

Notice that the first two paragraphs are a paragroup. A beginning writer would very likely be timid about using four paragraphs to give three examples. Yet the second paragraph helps call attention to an idea that runs through the next two paragraphs and is echoed by the word *visions* in Sentence 14.

You have seen various ways of emphasizing important ideas—by using summary sentences, linking expressions, paragroups, and space. Experienced writers use these ways in any combination that gives the desired emphasis to their ideas. In general, they follow the principle of saying the most about the things they consider of most importance.

Improving paragraphs
7. Have I used space wisely?

A reader judges to some extent the relative importance of your ideas by the amount of space you allocate to each of them. Once you realize this, you have a basis for deciding whether you have used space wisely. While the proportion of space allocated to each part of a composition is often only a rough guide, there are certain principles that may be helpful: (1) Paragraphs of approximately the same length may be used to express ideas of equal importance. (2) Short paragraphs may be used for unimportant ideas or those you think the reader already knows. (3) Long paragraphs or paragroups may be used for important ideas, those you particularly want the reader to understand and remember.

In revising first drafts of your compositions, always take time to ask yourself questions like these: Have I given enough space to important ideas? Have I used too much space for ideas that are unimportant or obvious? Such questions may suggest changes to make your composition more effective.

Remember that it is the proportion of space allocated to the various ideas that indicates their relative importance. For example, if you have told all you know about an important idea, you can hardly be expected to give it more space. But you can make it seem more prominent by using less space for other ideas. Explaining unimportant ideas briefly helps direct the reader's attention to those ideas you particularly want him to understand and remember.

Getting Off to a Good Start

As you know, an introductory paragraph is rarely used in a short composition of fifteen to twenty sentences. But in compositions of fifteen to twenty paragraphs, or longer, an introductory paragraph is not out of proportion and often helps the writer get off to a good start. While the purpose is the same as with an opening sentence—to arouse the reader's interest—two problems are always present. If the introduction is not closely related in thought with the rest of the composition, the reader will feel that he has been tricked. If it is not closely linked with the following paragraph, the reader will have trouble making the transition. Notice how both of these problems have been met in the following example:

> (1) It is not always easy in these days of rapid advance to distinguish what has already been achieved from what is yet to come. (2) Sometimes the newspapers herald almost as an accomplished fact a giant electronic brain that has only passed from being a gleam in an enthusiastic worker's eye to being a chronic pain in a discouraged worker's neck. (3) What predictions can be made about future developments in electronics?
>
> (4) Some things we can see rather clearly in a general way. . . .

Sentences 1 and 2 provide a background for the important question in Sentence 3. Sentence 4 echoes this question by partly answering it and so links the introduction to the next paragraph. (The dots following Sentence 4 indicate that the rest of the paragraph has been omitted.)

Sometimes an unusual incident makes a good beginning:

(1) Not long ago a Connecticut baker of specialty bread received a letter from a customer in Arizona. (2) There was nothing so very unusual about the distance of the customer. (3) Like many specialty bakers this one regularly sends orders to faraway enthusiasts who can afford such whims, and he frequently receives glowing testimonials from them. (4) But this particular letter struck a brand-new note.

(5) The customer—a lady naturalist—reported that she had made a pet of a red-winged blackbird. (6) One day she fed him crumbs of the baker's special bread. (7) The following day she spread before him crumbs of another type of bread.

(8) "He flatly refused to touch them," she concluded, "and scolded me angrily until I gave him your bread."

(9) This is the first indication that any of our furred or feathered friends of the animal kingdom have joined us in our more and more choosy attitude toward the staff of life. . . .

By telling about the fussy blackbird, the writer leads the reader into an árticle about bread. Notice that Sentences 1-8, explaining the incident, are a paragroup which is closely linked to the next paragraph by the pronoun *This* and the echo words *furred or feathered friends of the animal kingdom, choosy attitude,* and *the staff of life.*

Another common way of beginning is to give a striking fact that is likely to attract the reader's attention. For example:

(1) Try to imagine eight hundred guests trooping into your home every day and thoroughly inspecting each corner of it. (2) Then try to imagine having only two hours—from eight to ten in the morning—to ready the house for that day's visitors. (3) This is what faces Mrs. Joseph N. van Buren, head housekeeper of the Governor's Palace and other exhibition buildings at Colonial Williamsburg, Virginia, where it's open house every day of the year except Christmas.

(4) All the rooms in the buildings we visited had a calmly poised air—as though confidently expecting the arrival of guests—and we wondered how this effect had been achieved in two hours. (5) Then we wondered if the same methods might be useꞋd to keep a home as neat.

118

Here the first paragraph states the fact, while the second leads the reader directly into the article. Repetition of the words *buildings, guests, home,* and *two hours* also helps link the paragraphs.

Occasionally the whole first paragraph may be used just to arouse the reader's curiosity, as in this next example:

> (1) Barbed wire and staples, spikes and bits of chicken wire—gulp!—an old axe head and a half-dozen metal syrup spiles—in they go! (2) How would you like to watch a scythe blade or a broken piece of crosscut saw being eaten? (3) You can; it's going on every day. (4) It sounds sensational, doesn't it?
>
> (5) For the last fourteen years I've been watching a sugar maple swallow a porcelain insulator, and sometime, about 1975, it should finish it! (6) That's the trouble with trees; they don't swallow things fast enough to make it really exciting.

The strange diet suggested in the opening paragraph is frankly intended to lead the reader into the second paragraph. Notice that the two paragraphs are also tied together by the use of the words *watch* and *watching, being eaten* and *swallow.*

An unusual or exciting incident often makes a good beginning:

> (1) The hunter dismounted from his horse and proceeded cautiously on foot through the dense brush. (2) For thirty minutes he stalked his prey, circling until he sighted it in heavy underbrush and mesquite. (3) He took careful aim and fired.
>
> (4) His horse dropped dead.
>
> (5) It is careless and tragic enough to lose a fine horse, but how about the hunter in western New York who killed three hunters with one bullet last year?

As you can see, the first two paragraphs are a paragroup. By setting Sentence 4 off as a separate paragraph, the writer gives it added emphasis. Notice that Sentence 5 echoes the idea expressed in Sentence 4 and links it with tragic accidents involving hunters.

When space permits, an incident reported all or in part by dialogue almost always attracts the reader's attention:

(1) "I wonder if it's cool enough for a jacket?" inquired a young woman at an evening lawn party last summer.

(2) "Just a minute," I volunteered, "and I'll give you the temperature."

(3) I gazed at my watch a few seconds, then advised her. (4) "The temperature is 72 degrees. (5) Hardly cool enough for a jacket—or is it?"

(6) She thought I had a tiny thermometer on my watch and wanted to see it. (7) But I had merely timed a tree cricket that was chirping in the nearby shrubbery. (8) I had counted his chirps for 7 seconds, doubled the number, and added 16, which gave me the air temperature.

(9) The crickets are the best known of all insects in respect to their response to temperature and temperature changes. (10) Indeed, one cricket has come to be known as the Temperature Cricket. . . .

While the main part of the article actually begins with Sentence 9, the introduction is so closely linked to it by repetition of the word *temperature* that the reader is scarcely aware of the transition.

You have seen some of the ways in which writers use introductory paragraphs to arouse the reader's interest. When such paragraphs are carefully chosen, kept in proportion to the rest of the composition, and closely linked with it, they frequently entice the reader into looking over an article he might otherwise have ignored.

Improving paragraphs
8. Do I need an introductory paragraph?

Good salesmen try to win the attention of their customers before pointing out the merits of the product. Skilled speakers usually tell a joke or two before plunging into a serious talk. And experienced writers often use an introductory paragraph to arouse the reader's interest in what they have written. All realize the value of whetting a person's appetite before serving the main course.

A sense of proportion is, of course, necessary. A salesman cannot spend half of his interview winning attention and still do justice to his product. Nor can a speaker spend most of his time telling jokes and still do justice to his subject. When you use an introductory paragraph, always ask yourself: Do I really need a paragraph to arouse the reader's interest? Would an opening sentence perhaps be adequate? Is the paragraph in proportion to the rest of my composition?

Necessary, too, is a sense of fitness. Any salesman can win attention by being rude and quarrelsome, but he is not likely to make a sale. And unless a speaker's jokes have some connection with his subject, you feel that he is more interested in making you laugh than in expressing his ideas. Always test an introductory paragraph by asking yourself: Will the reader see the connection between my opening paragraph and the rest of my composition? How well does it prepare him for what I am going to say?

A sense of responsibility also helps. Having won favorable attention, salesman and speaker alike try to get down to business promptly. Always ask yourself: Have I linked my introductory paragraph closely to the following paragraphs? Have I been careful to lead the reader into the next part of my composition?

As you have seen, introductory paragraphs are of many kinds—some explaining or describing a situation, others giving interesting facts or statistics, still others relating an anecdote or an unusual incident. Whatever kind you choose, be sure that it is in keeping with the rest of your composition and leads naturally into it. Though sometimes written last, or even added during revision, a good introductory paragraph gives the impression of being an essential part of the whole composition.

EXERCISE 7. In a magazine you read regularly, find an interesting article that has a good introduction of one or more paragraphs. Read through the article carefully. On a sheet of paper, write the name of the author, the title of the article, the name of the magazine, and its date. Then copy the introduction. Below it, write a few sentences telling briefly what the article is about and why you think the introduction is good. Be ready to read the introduction to your classmates and to discuss your opinion of it with them.

Summarizing
Important Ideas

When we look at the skyline of a large city, we are inclined to notice certain buildings of distinctive size or shape. Because they stand out clearly from the rest, such buildings are landmarks that often help identify the city and plainly distinguish its skyline from those of other cities.

In almost every composition certain ideas are more important than others. When these important ideas are made to stand out clearly, they help the reader grasp the central thought of the composition and remember it accurately. A summarizing paragraph is one way of giving prominence to such ideas.

Earlier you learned that a summary sentence may be used to restate the central idea of a paragraph. In a similar way, a single sentence may be used to sum up the important ideas in a whole composition. Here, for example, is the final paragraph from an article recommending winter travel in Switzerland:

> So whether it's for the wonders of winter scenery, for elfin nostalgia, for robust snow sports, or for the sheer creature comforts of a nation which has learned how to cater to tourists, we give you Switzerland for January.

Each of the phrases beginning with *for* refers to an important idea expressed in one of the four preceding paragraphs, while the main clause sums up "in a nutshell" the central thought of the article. The sentence is set off as a separate paragraph to show that it summarizes important ideas from all the paragraphs, not just the fourth.

While final paragraphs of one sentence are fairly common, most summarizing paragraphs consist of two or more sentences. Here, for example, is one of four sentences from an eighteen-paragraph article on ways of controlling hatred and directing it to useful ends:

> Can you afford to hate? Certainly you cannot afford to
> hate unwisely. Whenever you are tempted to hate your fellow
> human beings, remember, "Let him who is without sin cast
> the first stone." Then get busy and hate the evils in the world
> that need correcting—and hate them enough to help correct
> them.

By repeating the title of his article, the writer emphasizes the problem.
By suggesting two solutions, he makes his important ideas stand out
clearly without itemizing them in detail.

The number of sentences in a summarizing paragraph is determined more by the writer's ideas and what he wishes to say about
them than by the length of his composition. For example, here are
four sentences used to sum up a long article of thirty-six paragraphs
about famine conditions in India:

> For at least two centuries the world's production of food
> has increased faster than its population; but within the last
> few years the situation appears to have been reversed, and the
> population of the world has increased faster than its food
> supply. The world is moving toward the condition that India
> has already reached. India has many lessons for us. It would
> be well to help and to study India.

In the first two sentences of this summarizing paragraph the writer
restates important ideas explained in his article. In the last two he
points out their significance to his readers.

Summarizing paragraphs are not always at the end of a composition. They may also be used after any part of it to call attention to
important ideas. For example, here are four paragraphs from a long
article on the migration of birds. Notice that the fourth is a summarizing paragraph:

> How do birds find their way, particularly when traveling
> by night—yes, even through dense fogs—or when crossing
> great bodies of water? Many return to the same nesting
> ground every year. The greater shearwater moves unerringly
> from the North Atlantic to its only breeding place, a small

island in the South Atlantic about midway between Africa and South America.

Undoubtedly birds depend somewhat upon their eyesight, many theorists believing that birds fly "contact" as do aviators, by following known objects upon the ground. According to these thinkers, the old birds lead the young ones over the route to be followed, and this guided trip is sufficient to fix its pattern in their minds. But this is certainly not true in the case of the western sandpipers, at least, for the young birds do not migrate until a month after their parents.

Sense of sight, however, cannot function when flying through dense fogs, or over a vast stretch of water. Even if a bird's eyesight were infinite in reach, it still would not serve in some cases. When the ruby throat sets out to fly the Gulf of Mexico, even if this dauntless little aviator started at an altitude of five miles it still could not see over the earth's curvature between itself and Mexico.

Thus, in spite of research, scientists still face the facts of migration with a sense of frustration, mingled with hope. Birds must carry in their heads, in addition to their other special senses, that which for want of a better term we may call a sense of direction.

The writer might have ended this part of his composition with the third paragraph, which makes it clear that sense of sight alone does not explain the mystery of migration. But by summing up the result of the conflict in viewpoints, the writer makes it easier for readers to agree with the explanation he suggests.

Sometimes a summarizing paragraph is used to make quite clear what the writer means, as in these three paragraphs at the beginning of an article on the relationship of discipline and freedom:

> The good driver brings his car to a full halt at the boulevard stop sign. He does this because he is properly disciplined. He is disciplined by *know-how*, by *know-why*, and by *want-right*. He knows how to handle his car. He knows why the stop sign is needed. He wants to obey the stop regulation because he believes it is right. His driving discipline supports and extends his freedom and the freedom of other drivers

and of pedestrians to travel more safely than would be possible without discipline.

The poor driver may fail to obey the stop sign. He does so because he lacks one or more of the elements of good discipline in the situation. He does not know how to bring his car to a halt correctly. For example, he may step on the accelerator instead of the brake. He may not know why he should stop. Or he may know very well how and why to stop but just lacks the desire to do what he knows is the right thing to do. He is undisciplined, and his own freedom, as well as the freedom of others to move safely, is thereby curtailed.

This view of discipline as essential to freedom can be similarly illustrated in any activity of men in groups. To get a job done as smartly and smoothly as possible, the group develops patterns of action. The individual's freedom to act with the group is not restricted but enhanced by acquiring the discipline of those patterns.

Without the third paragraph you might think that the writer was telling about good and poor drivers. But with it you know that the first two paragraphs are intended merely as specific examples illustrating an abstract idea. Notice that the summarizing paragraph states this idea in a general way and shows how it applies to other groups.

Summarizing paragraphs may consist of one sentence or more. They may occur at the end of a composition or after any part of it. And as you have seen, they are often an effective way of giving special emphasis to ideas that the writer considers of particular importance.

Improving paragraphs
9. Do I need a summarizing paragraph?

Whether or not you use an introductory paragraph often depends on the length of your composition. Whether or not you use a summarizing paragraph is more likely to depend on the content. If you are telling about something that happened or something you have seen, a closing sentence may be adequate, no matter how many paragraphs there are. But if you are expressing an opinion or telling what something means, a summarizing paragraph may improve your composition, even though it is short. When you are trying to decide, ask yourself: Will a summarizing paragraph help the reader understand my meaning? Do I want to call his attention to the important ideas? If the answers are Yes, you probably need a summarizing paragraph.

Most of the paragraphs you have studied tend to advance the thought of a composition. Each new paragraph is another step along the way, taking up another phase of the subject, adding more facts or opinions or examples. Even introductory paragraphs, whose main purpose is to attract the attention of the reader, ordinarily lead him into the paragraphs that follow.

A summarizing paragraph is different. It has the effect of saying to the reader, "The ideas expressed in the preceding paragraphs are important. Let's stop for a moment to make certain that we understand their meaning." By bringing the reader to a halt in this way, you encourage him to think over what he has just read. You also direct his attention emphatically to whatever you wish to say about it. For this reason, only important ideas belong in a summarizing paragraph.

There are many ways of summing up such ideas so that the reader will realize their importance. You may simply restate them to show "in a nutshell" what you mean. You may analyze them, evaluate them, point out their significance, make a general comment about them, or tie them up with the opening paragraph to emphasize the central thought of your composition. Whatever your choice, you will do well to refer only to ideas that have been previously explained. A "new" idea is out of place in a summarizing paragraph. No matter how clear its relationship with the others may be in your mind, it is likely to confuse or distract the reader.

As you revise a composition containing a summarizing paragraph, ask yourself questions like these: Have I included in the summarizing paragraph the ideas that I particularly want the reader to remember? Have I shown why they are important? Have I been careful to exclude ideas that have not been previously explained? Such questions will remind you that the purpose of a summarizing paragraph is to call the reader's attention to important ideas in preceding paragraphs.

EXERCISE 8. In a magazine you read regularly, find an interesting article that has an effective summarizing paragraph. Read through the article carefully. On a sheet of paper, write the name of the author, the title of the article, the name of the magazine, and its date. Then copy the summarizing paragraph. Below it, write a few sentences telling briefly what the article is about and why you think the summarizing paragraph effective. Be ready to read the paragraph to your classmates and to discuss it with them.

Bridging the Gaps

You have learned that linking expressions are useful in helping readers follow the writer's thought as it moves from paragraph to paragraph. When the paragraphs are closely related, as they usually are in a short composition, the gap in thought is narrow; and a few words are sufficient to help the reader across it. But if the gap is wide, as it sometimes is in going from one part of a long composition to another, several sentences may be needed to help the reader make the transition. A paragraph consisting of such sentences is a **transitional paragraph**.

Here, for example, are four paragraphs from an article on the importance of staying healthy. The first paragraph ends one part of the article. The third introduces another part. As you read the selection, see if you are conscious of the wide gap in thought between the two:

(1) How about the way you walk? (2) The right walk is free and easy—toes pointed forward, legs moving close together, knees limber, body in easy balance—with head, shoulders, and hips in line. (3) Try it and see how much more comfortable and graceful it is than a head-forward stride, a toeing-out waddle, or a stiff pavement-pounding tread.

(4) So far we've been discussing health mostly in relation to personality and prettiness. (5) But that word "health" is the great common denominator, as your math teacher would say, for personality, prettiness, and patriotism as well. (6) Isn't it a happy coincidence that you can also serve your country while you are serving yourself?

(7) Why is it so patriotic to be healthy?

(8) We'll start with the most practical consideration. (9) You probably have read or heard about the shortage of doctors and nurses in this country. (10) Even in normal times, there just aren't enough to go around. . . .

Notice how the second paragraph bridges the gap between the first and third paragraphs. Sentence 4 sums up the preceding part of the article. Sentence 5 adds a new idea—patriotism. Sentence 6 ties this new idea in with the rest of the article, so that readers can follow the thought as it moves from personal to national aspects of the subject. As you can see, the three sentences work together as a transitional paragraph.

Somewhat different is the transitional paragraph that links two parts of a composition by combining the end of one part with the beginning of the next one. As you read the following selection, notice the way in which the third paragraph ties together the second and fourth ones:

(1) Young hearts ache when intimate friendships break up. (2) Boys and girls of teen age feel almost destroyed when close relationships swiftly cool and wane. (3) Perhaps young people invest so great a portion of themselves in a friendship that everything seems lost when one partner puts the other one back into circulation.

(4) Girls are more inclined than boys to show outward signs of this inner hurt. (5) But boys feel just as injured and miserable over being let down by once ardent friends. (6) Most boys learn early to cover inner feelings with an outer layer of bravado. (7) I have come to have a special respect for the girl or boy who takes the break-up of a friendship with a smile and says, "Well, there are other fish in the sea. (8) I'll just have to find a new pal. (9) Wish me luck!"

(10) That kind of spunk is good. (11) It carries you over the period of shock moderately well. (12) It gives you the needed breather while you get your emotional feet under you again. (13) The next big thing you need to do is to stop a moment and ask yourself, "Why do friends drop me?"

(14) There may be several practical answers in your own case. (15) One factor that almost certainly is mixed up in the problem is that your interests and attitudes have changed considerably in the past year. (16) The interests and attitudes of the other fellow probably have changed just as much as yours—though not necessarily in the same direction. . . .

If you look carefully at the third paragraph, you will see that Sentences 10, 11, and 12 are a sort of summary for the second paragraph, while Sentence 13 introduces the next part of the article. By combining Sentence 13 with the other three, the writer not only bridges the gap between the two parts, but also shows that they are closely related in his mind.

You have seen that transitional paragraphs, like linking expressions, are useful in helping readers follow a writer's thought. And you have learned that by summing up what has come before and by preparing readers for what comes next, such paragraphs can bridge wider gaps in thought than linking expressions can. But you should also remember that a composition may have a half-dozen parts, each of several paragraphs, and still not need a single transitional paragraph. It is not the number of parts a composition has that determines the need for a transitional paragraph, but the difficulty readers may have in going from one part to the next. Skilled writers use a transitional paragraph only when they feel it is needed to make clear the meaning they intend.

Improving paragraphs
10. Have I kept the reader in mind?

In some newspaper offices it is customary for an editorial writer to keep on his desk a snapshot of an utter stranger—a laboring man in overalls, a housewife carrying a bag of groceries, or some other person representing a typical reader of the paper. This is not done for any sentimental reason, of course, but simply to remind the writer constantly of his readers so that he will write his editorials for them, not for himself.

Keeping the reader in mind at all times is probably the most valuable habit a writer can form. Certainly it helps him greatly in planning, writing, and revising any composition with ideas in it, ideas that he wants to communicate to others. From selecting suitable details to using transitional paragraphs, he must constantly be thinking of his readers, putting himself in their place, trying in every way to help them understand what he wants them to know. Only as he learns to assume this responsibility, can he hope to acquire skill in expressing his thoughts effectively.

Particularly in revising first drafts for meaning is it important to keep the reader in mind. To help you, the suggestions for improving paragraphs have been phrased as questions. As you review them here, notice how many can be satisfactorily answered only by thinking of yourself as the reader, only by putting yourself in his place and anticipating the difficulties he might have in understanding you. In this way you have been learning to assume your share of responsibility for effective communication.

1. **Have I selected details carefully?**
2. **Have I explained details adequately?**
3. **Do I need a general statement?**
4. **Do I need a summary sentence?**
5. **Have I used good linking expressions?**
6. **Have I grouped details effectively?**
7. **Have I used space wisely?**
8. **Do I need an introductory paragraph?**
9. **Do I need a summarizing paragraph?**
10. **Have I kept the reader in mind?**

As you may recall, the first five suggestions have to do mostly with individual paragraphs, while the last five are concerned more with paragraphs as parts of the whole composition.

Answers to the Exercises in "Working With Paragraphs"

Exercise **1** *Page* **80** Selecting details

The revised letter will probably be similar to the following:

I would have written sooner, but we've been visiting at Uncle Ed's farm. It's a dairy farm, and there are lots of cows. The barn is about a block long, with concrete floors and fluorescent lights and everything painted white. It looks like a hospital. The house is a huge, rambling, two-story affair with wide screened-in porches, a big stone fireplace, and rooms about the size of our classrooms at school. The kitchen is enormous, about right for a restaurant; and opening off the dining room is a large screened-in porch where we eat our breakfasts.

Uncle Ed is over fifty, but full of pep, and hasn't a gray hair on his head. He's a big man and likes a lot of space to move around in. He is more fun than a circus—always laughing and thinking up things for us to do. One afternoon he took us fishing, and Dad caught two big brook trout. That made him feel good, particularly since Uncle Ed had no luck at all. But he just laughed about it and kidded Dad about "beginner's luck." He promised to take me along in his plane the next time he flies to town. He says the farmers out here use planes about the same way we use cars at home.

The trip out was pretty tiring. We started as early as we could every morning and drove until dark. I'll never forget driving through the mountains. The scenery was wonderful.

We'll probably be staying here for at least another week or so before starting back. That ought to be the latter part of August. Let's hope the return trip will be less tiresome.

Some students may include one or more of the following sentences in their revised letters. The sentences have been omitted in this revision.

I've even learned the difference between Holstein and Jersey cows!
So there just wasn't any time to write letters.
Did you know that the cream from Jersey cows is almost as yellow as butter?
We have it on our cereal every morning.
It's so thick Dad says you ought to spread it on instead of trying to pour it!
Uncle Ed's house is as big as a barn—not his barn, of course, but the kind we see around home.
. . . but Aunt Nelly says it takes a lot of cooking to keep Unicle Ed filled up.
It surely must save a lot of time, and there are plenty of places to land.
I'll tell you all about it when I get back home.

Exercise **2** *Page* **85** Improving sentences in paragraphs

Suggested revisions of the sentences are:

(1, 2, 3,) Rainsford lay in his chair on the deck of the yacht, puffing at his favorite pipe and thinking over the venest of the past week. (4, 5, 6) Just as he grew (*or* was growing) drowsy, a sharp sound off to the right startled him. (7, 8) His ears, trained to that sort of sound, could not be mistaken. (9) Again he heard the sound. (10) Somewhere off in the darkness of the night someone had fired a gun.

(11, 12, 13) Mystified, Rainsford sprang up and moved quickly to the rail. (14, 15) Although he strained his eyes, he could not see at all through the dense blackness. (16, 17, 18, 19) When he jumped up on the rail, thinking he might see better from there, his pipe struck a rope and was knocked out of his mouth. (20, 21, 22) Lunging for it, he stretched too far and lost his balance.

(23, 24, 25) As the warm waters of the Caribbean Sea closed over his head, he struggled to the surface, shouting wildly. (26, 27) But the wash of the yacht, slapping against his face, made him gag and strangle.

(28, 29) In desperation he struck out after the lights of the yacht, which were receding rapidly. (30, 31, 32, 33) He swam frantically for about fifty feet and then stopped, knowing that he had to calm his excited nerves. (34, 35) Since this was not the first time he had been in a tight place, he quickly regained his self-possession.

(36) Then he had to decide what to do next. (37, 38, 39, 40) Realizing that there was a slight chance that someone on the yacht was still on deck and might hear his cries, he shouted with all his power for several minutes. (41) No one heard him. (42, 43) The lights of the yacht grew fainter and soon were blotted out by the night.

Exercise **3**   *Page* **91**   Writing general statements

The general statements you students write should be similar to the following:

1 a) Wisconsin, the land of lakes, is famous not only for its resorts, but also for its dairying industry and livestock production.
 b) The people of Wisconsin are justly proud of their state.
2 a) Although the competition is keen, amateur boxing is a safe, well-regarded sport.
 b) Amateur boxing differs from professional boxing in several respects.
3 a) Television has brought benefits both to the people who watch and to those who perform.
 b) With a twist of the dial, the TV viewer can choose from a variety of entertainment.

Suggested revisions of the sentences are:

(1, 2) There are many strange foreign foods that we consider unappetizing. (3, 4) Though we shudder at the thought of eating such foods, native connoisseurs consider them rare delicacies (*or* they are considered rare delicacies by native connoisseurs). (5, 6, 7, 8) Among these unusual foods are such exotic dishes as shark-fin soup; snails in vinegar; African black ants, which are deep fried; and sea-slugs.

(9, 10) In America we are particular about one thing—having our eggs fresh. (11) In China fermented eggs are highly esteemed. (12, 13, 14) These eggs, buried for long periods of time, become green and cheeselike. (15, 16) The older the eggs are, the more flavorful they are considered—and the more valuable, too. (17, 18) In the homes of the very wealthy, eggs one hundred years old might be served.

(19, 20) Another Chinese luxury is bird's-nest soup, made from the nests of a species of swifts. (21, 22) These swifts build their homes high on the faces of cliffs and at the mouths of caves. (23, 24) The nests are made of twigs and seaweed, which the birds glue together with their saliva. (25, 26) The twigs and seaweed are strained out and discarded, and the saliva is used in bird's-nest soup. (27, 28, 29) Since the nests are very hard to get and their cost is extremely great, none except the rich can afford this rare delicacy.

(30, 31) We Americans like our tea with lemon or cream. (32, 33, 34, 35, 36) The Tartars and Tibetans of central Asia prefer butter in their tea—a reeking, rancid butter made from yak's milk. (37, 38, 39) The Oriental uses this butter on his cigarettes too, causing them to splutter in burning and making them emit a choking and pungent smoke.

(40, 41) To us these strange habits and strange foods are revolting and disgusting. (42, 43, 44) But many Americans eat raw clams, rattlesnake meat, and sweetbreads, considering them treats to delight the palate of a gourmet. (45) Maybe taste is just a matter of geography.